Living the
Success Principles

Inspiring Stories
of Real People Achieving
Extraordinary Results

COMPILED AND EDITED BY

Jack Canfield

Publisher: The Canfield Training Group
P.O. Box 30880
Santa Barbara, CA 93130

Email: *Info@JackCanfield.com*
Phone: 805-881-5191
FAX: 805-563-2945

Cover design by Larissa Hise Henoch

CONTENTS

ACKNOWLEDGMENTS

I wish to acknowledge the following people:

All the people who so generously wrote and contributed their stories of personal and professional transformation to this book. Your courage and commitment to living the success principles is an inspiration to all of us.

Carol Kline, who interviewed many of the people whose stories appear in this book and who crafted those interviews into the moving stories you are about to read. Without Carol's brilliant interviewing and editing skills this book would never have been completed. Thank you, Carol.

Patty Aubery, who first encouraged me to write the book *The Success Principles: How to Get from Where You Are to Where You Want to Be*, without which this work never would have attracted all the people whose stories are contained in this book. You have been an amazing business partner and friend.

Janet Switzer, who coauthored *The Success Principles* and the *10th Anniversary Revised Edition of The Success Principles* with me. Janet, you are an incredible friend, colleague and writer who has been with me throughout this journey.

Stephen Hanselman, the former editor at HarperCollins who championed the publication of the first edition and the revised edition of *The Success Principles*.

Bonnie Solow, my literary agent at the time who convinced Stephen and everyone else at HarperCollins to believe in the original Success Principles book.

Kim Kirberger, my sister and the coauthor of most of the *Chicken Soup for the Teenage Soul* books, who helped me sort through many of the stories that were submitted for inclusion in this book.

Russ Kamalski, the CEO of the Canfield Training Group, who keeps everything running smoothly so that I have the time and support to compile and edit these books.

Veronica Romero, my executive assistant, without whom none of this would get done. She keeps me sane in another wise crazy world. Thanks, Roni, for making sure everything works, running the office, and keeping the wolves at bay. You are the best.

My wonderful wife Inga, who loves and supports me and stands by me when I go into these long periods of writing and editing and spending less time with her than she would like. I appreciate your understanding and supporting my mission in the world. I love you!

Alice, Jesse, Kajsa, Lisa, Jody, Donna, Lexi, Teresa, and Dwain— my incredibly loyal and productive staff, whose efforts make all the seminars, trainings, websites, podcasts, newsletters, blogs, social media, PR, marketing, sales, customer service, accounting and everything else that it takes to support the hundreds of thousands of students and clients we have around the world actually work. Thanks so much.

Mike Hussey, Roger Sinnes, Dahlia Fukuda, Koran Messina, Chris Lecheminant, Wade Lindstrom, John Beaman, Gary Reid

and all the great Canfield Coaching staff at the Professional Education Institute. You are the secret sauce that have helped thousands of our coaching clients all over the world apply the success principles and achieve their dreams.

Peter Vegso and all our friends at Health Communications Inc. for printing this book in record time. Thanks for your commitment to publishing books that make a difference in the world.

INTRODUCTION

This first edition of *Living the Success Principles* is a collection of stories by people who have successfully gone from where they were to where they wanted to be as a result of applying the principles and strategies for breakthrough success that they learned when they read *The Success Principles*, attended my five-day Breakthrough to Success Training, graduated from my Train the Trainer Program, worked with one of my Canfield Coaches, attended one of our private luxury retreats, watched or listened to one of my audiovisual programs, or saw me in the movie "The Secret."

I hope that when you read these stories of ordinary people who have accomplished extraordinary things by actively applying the transformational principles they learned, that you will be inspired to learn and apply the proven success principles that I teach to your life and your career so that you too can create breakthrough results in all the areas of your life.

You can learn more about our trainings, our coaching program, and all of our books and audio and video programs at: *www.JackCanfield.com*, or by contacting one of our staff at 805-881-5191.

THE MAGIC OF VISUALIZING

Kabir Khan

I was six years old when I found my life's calling. It was the night I saw the world's greatest magician, David Copperfield, perform on television.

That year he was coming to Malaysia, and to promote his tour, there was a program about him on TV. The night of the program, my dad and mom and I ate a quick dinner and settled in front of the TV in the living room of our apartment in Kuala Lumpur.

I remember watching, my eyes wide with amazement, as the American magician did trick after trick, each more incredible than the last. Then, as the grand finale, he made a huge green statue in America—what my parents called the Statue of Liberty— disappear. I'd seen clowns make balloons and trinkets disappear, but a national monument? Overcome with wonder, I felt something click into place inside me. I thought, *That's what I want to do. I want to be a magician.*

For days, all I could talk about was the magic show. A few weeks later, my parents bought me a magic kit that had a device in it that made coins vanish. I spent hours in my room practicing. When I turned 11, my mother bought me a full set of magic equipment, and I started doing shows for my friends, performing at birthday parties and even at my school.

As the years passed, my goals became more ambitious. I longed to train with the best magicians in the world—all of whom were in America. How could I get there? My family didn't have a lot of money and besides, they thought my magic was a nice hobby but expected me to pursue a normal career. So after high school, I attended college and studied marketing. But I also kept my dream alive by performing regularly at one of the large hotels in Kuala Lumpur. Then for my 20th birthday, I received a copy of Jack Canfield's book, *The Success Principles*.

From the very first page, I was hooked. I felt like Jack was talking directly to me. His ideas were so easy to understand and they rang true. My special treat was to come home in the evening after my classes and read the book and think about how I could apply the teachings. When I saw in the paper one day that Jack was coming to Kuala Lumpur, I knew I had to see him. My parents, aware of my enthusiasm for Jack and his work, kindly offered to help me buy the ticket.

At the course, I stood up and told Jack about my dream of being a world-class magician. Jack smiled at me and said, "That's great! Now, let's figure out what you need to do to make that dream come true."

He talked about writing down my goals, creating a vision board, using affirmations, taking 100% responsibility for my life. These were all things I had read about in *The Success Principles*, but for some reason I had been holding back from putting them into action. Now I dove in!

One of the principles Jack recommends is "Act as if." He writes, " . . . [A]ct as if you are already where you want to be. This means thinking like, dressing like, acting like, and feeling like the person who has already achieved your goal." Now I asked myself, *If I were already a world-famous magician, how would I act? What would I wear? Where would I shop?* I thought of David Copperfield—of course, he would go only to the best stores. So I took the train to the high-end mall and strolled around. I saw a shop displaying beautiful watches of all types. *Would a world-class magician wear a cheap watch?* I asked myself. *No way!*

I walked into the store and looked in all the cases. One watch, made by a Swiss company called Fortis, really attracted me. The clerk said it was a watch that astronauts wore. I asked if I could try it on. As soon as I placed it on my wrist, I fell in love with the feel of it; it was so solid and well-made. But it cost $3,000! I didn't have that kind of money.

Using my cell phone, I took a picture of the watch, still on my wrist. Then I took it off and handed it back to the clerk, thinking, *Take care of this for me till I come back and buy it.*

At home, I printed out the photo and pasted it on my vision board. I decided not to wear a watch until I could wear the Fortis, so I removed my plastic watch and began using my cell phone to tell the time. Remembering Jack's instructions, I made a point to look at the picture of the Fortis on my wrist each day. Every so often, I went back to the store to visit my watch and make sure it was still there. The clerks at the store ignored me, knowing I wasn't yet ready to buy, but I didn't mind. I never doubted for an instant that I would own that watch someday.

About six months after Jack's workshop, things began to pop: I found a group willing to pay for me to go to magic school in America! But my joy was short-lived, because after more consideration, the group decided that I was too young. They told me I should finish college and then come back and ask again. I was devastated—and humiliated. I'd told all my friends that I was going to America. Now what would I say?

I stayed at home for a few days, feeling terrible, then read in the paper that Jack was scheduled to give another talk in Kuala Lumpur the very next day. I immediately went to the hotel where I thought he'd be staying and sat in the lobby, holding my copy of *The Success Principles* and scanning each new arrival coming through the door. Six hours went by with no sign of Jack, but I wouldn't give up. Finally, I saw him come in. I jumped up from my seat and walked over to him, holding up my book. "Jack," I said, "I need your help."

He took one look at me and, recognizing me from his last visit, said, "Okay, come up to my suite. Let's talk."

In Jack's suite, I told him my story. He listened carefully and when I was finished he said, "You've done well, Kabir, but you need to refine your goals. Don't say, 'I want to study magic in America.' Say, 'I *am* studying magic in America.' Change your vision board to reflect this. Use images and phrases that create the feeling of already having what you want."

Jack went on, reminding me to believe in myself. "Keep on going!" he said. "Remember principles 17 and 18, 'Ask, ask, ask,' and 'Reject rejection'? Remember, there are a million people out there. If you don't get your yes—you just haven't asked the right person yet."

After Jack's pep talk, I was on fire. I began asking everyone I could think of to sponsor me to study in America: businessmen, community leaders, even the prime minister! I was relentless. And to keep myself accountable, I emailed Jack regularly with progress reports.

Not long after my talk with Jack, I met a successful Chinese businessman named Mr. Wong, who seemed interested in my pursuit of my dream. Mr. Wong was the friend of a friend, and the three of us decided to start a mastermind group together. To my delight, Mr. Wong invited three of his business colleagues to join us as well. We planned to discuss our goals and our progress towards achieving them, and offer each other support and advice. We treated these meetings as serious business and met in a top-quality hotel restaurant twice a month, wearing business suits and ties.

After our second meeting, out of the blue, Mr. Wong called me and offered to sponsor me. My father, astonished and perhaps a bit suspicious, invited Mr. Wong to our home so that he and my mother could meet him. After they had exchanged formalities, my father asked Mr. Wong why he was giving someone he'd known for only a month such a substantial amount of money. Mr. Wong said simply, "I believe in your son."

When I looked at the check he handed me, my eyes widened in surprise. It was for 80,000 Ringgit ($23,000)—20,000 Ringgit more than the amount I'd put on my vision board! With that money, I was able to go to the United States and attend magic school for a year, graduating with a certificate and an even fiercer desire to become a world-famous magician—the Malaysian David Copperfield!

Back in Kuala Lumpur, I began performing regularly in clubs throughout the country. My reputation soon spread and I began giving shows all over the Middle East and Asia. I was steadily gaining momentum toward my goal, but to really hit the big time, I knew I'd have to perform in the US—specifically at The Magic Castle in Hollywood and at a club or hotel in Las Vegas.

Now, The Magic Castle is a very prestigious venue for a magician. Only hand-picked magicians are allowed to perform there before its elite audience. My experience with Mr. Wong's check had convinced me of the power of visualizing, so I had a friend make a mock-up of a newspaper article with the headline: MALAYSIAN MAGICIAN TO PERFORM IN HOLLYWOOD. In the article, he included a photo of me and the news that I'd been invited to perform at The Magic Castle in Hollywood and also in Las Vegas.

I put this "article" on my vision board and took time every day to read it. Each time I'd make a point to experience the same feelings of gratitude and exhilaration I'd have if it were real. It got so that just walking by my vision board would make me smile, the joy of my accomplishments filling my heart.

The picture of the Fortis on my wrist was also still pinned up on my vision board and I included it in my daily visualization. Since returning from the States, I'd been continuing to save money toward purchasing it. With a generous gift from my family on my birthday, I finally had the amount I needed, and I set off to buy my watch. But when I walked into the shop, my heart stopped—the whole Fortis display was gone! The salesman told me that that line of watches wasn't selling well in Malaysia, so they'd stopped stocking them. Seeing my disappointment, the man said, "Hold on a sec. Let me just look in back." He returned with a pile of watches he said they offered to special clients in private shows and dumped them on the counter. There it was! My watch! I didn't think twice; I picked it up and put it on.

The clerk told me that, because it was discontinued, he would give me a big discount. So I paid just $1,000 for my dream watch! Magic was showing up in all areas of my life through the success principles I was practicing faithfully every day.

Then, in the summer of 2011, after a year of visualizing and doing other practices from the book, I received an invitation to perform at The Magic Castle. Wow! On the strength of that invitation, my agent booked a few engagements in Las Vegas nightclubs as well. All that was missing were enough funds to travel to the US and stay in hotels there; my fees wouldn't cover all my expenses—even using the money I'd saved on my watch. Determined not to let this opportunity slip away, I racked my brain for ways to raise the money.

That's when I had a brilliant idea. I picked up the phone and called the Fortis sales representative for Singapore, a man named Mr. Michael. He and I had become friends over the years as he had heard about my enthusiasm for my Fortis and my persistence in getting it. In fact, I had long considered myself an unofficial Fortis ambassador, having inspired a number of people—including Mr. Wong from my mastermind group—to purchase one.

Mr. Michael," I said, "It's confirmed! I'm going to be the first Malaysian magician to perform in Hollywood and Las Vegas! This could be a great opportunity for Fortis—would they like to sponsor my US tour?" Mr. Michael saw the potential of the idea immediately. He contacted the Fortis executives in Switzerland and called me back the next day to tell me the good news: They'd agreed to sponsor me! They knew it would bring Fortis good publicity and visibility, so it was a clear win/win. I was going to the U.S.A.!

The trip was fantastic and performing on stage at The Magic Castle and in the clubs in Las Vegas was every bit as exciting and fulfilling as I had imagined it would be. But one of the most satisfying moments of all happened before I even left Malaysia. Looking online at publicity for my upcoming trip to America, I couldn't believe my eyes when I saw the article about it on Yahoo News. I had been reading my made-up headline for months and there it was, but this time for real: MALAYSIAN MAGICIAN TO PERFORM IN HOLLYWOOD. I had done it! And quickly, too—I was only 26 years old.

My success as a magician is a big part of my story—I continue to perform internationally and even gave a recent command performance for the Sheikh of Dubai—but there's more. Mr. Wong and I are now business partners and have several exciting and lucrative projects together, including the iconic Revolving Restaurant at the famous Kuala Lumpur Tower, the 6th highest restaurant in the world!

I'm also pursuing new dreams: getting my private pilot's license, starting my own magic school so that I can mentor other young magicians, as well as my single biggest goal for this year, which is to be a guest on the Ellen DeGeneres show. I don't know how it will happen, but I've seen it in my mind and have already prepared three tricks to perform. Stay tuned . . . .

When I first learned magic, one of my favorite tricks was to make money disappear. Years later, Jack taught me another kind of magic, the kind that makes money—and fame, success, and happiness—appear! Today, I tell my audiences, "Magic is believing anything can happen."

LIVING THE DREAM

Raj Bhavsar

It was time.

I stood completely still, my body primed with adrenalin and my mind focusing fiercely, trying to forget the judges, the other gymnasts, and the huge arena I was in, as I prepared to launch myself upward and grab the rings. I'd done this routine hundreds, no, thousands of times before, but it had all come down to this moment.

I took a deep breath, and jumped. My hands clenched the hard fiberglass resin of the rings.

For the next few minutes, my mind was silent as I carefully maneuvered my body through a series of fluid moves with controlled precision. Then, releasing the rings, I swung up and over in a double-double layout (a double flip with a double twist in the layout position). As I landed on the mat, I felt my feet connect and then stick! I threw my arms above my head—my whole body upright, every muscle taut except for the corners of my mouth, which I felt pulling upward in a smile. Yes! I had nailed it!

The year was 2004, and I was competing for a spot on the U.S. Olympic gymnastics team. Of the 12 routines I'd done, 11, including this one, had been perfect. Everybody agreed: I was a shoo-in. Elated, I thought, *Greece, here I come!*

But at the conclusion of the trials, when they read off the names of the Olympians, mine wasn't on the list. Then I heard the words, "Raj Bhavsar, alternate."

I couldn't take it in. When I finally did, I was humiliated and angry. My world—everything I'd been working toward for a decade and a half—was shattered. For the next few years, I burned with one desire: to find out why I'd been denied. I needed to find someone to blame . . .

+ + + +

I was born to be a gymnast. It was the natural career choice for a kid who at the age of four lived to climb up things, like trees and furniture, and jump off of them. My parents, worried that I'd hurt myself and destroy our house, signed me up for gymnastics classes at a nearby gym. The jumps and movements I learned were fun and exciting, and I quickly fell in love with the sport.

I wasn't an all-star in the early days—I was bringing home a lot of purple and brown ribbons for 7th and 8th place finishes. But that didn't matter to my coaches, and it certainly didn't matter to me. I was lucky to have coaches who recognized my enthusiasm and drive, and nurtured my talent. By age 10, I'd set my sights on the Olympics. I wanted to be the best at this sport that I loved, and represent my country.

I began focusing intensely on becoming a better gymnast, and soon the successes began to show up. I started coming in first and second place at competitions and was a five-time Texas champion by the time I entered high school.

My parents were supportive of my interest in gymnastics—as long as it didn't compromise my academic performance. In fact, one of the main skills I learned as a kid was time management!

My high school and college years were a blur of awards and championships: Regional State Champion, National Champion, Senior National team, and then placement in two medal-winning championship teams. I was unstoppable. In my mind, I had the idea, "Oh, life is going to be like this for me. Going to the Olympics is just going to happen, because it's the next stop for this train." My expectations were sky-high and tangled up with my self-worth, so when they weren't met on that awful day in 2004, I came down to earth with a crash.

I went to Greece as an alternate, but it was a bittersweet experience watching my teammates work out together and compete day after day. Unofficially, I was part of the team, yet it was clear that I wasn't really one of them. I never had a chance to compete and I returned from the trip disillusioned and lost.

Back at home, I did some serious soul searching. I asked myself, *Do I truly enjoy gymnastics? Do I love the competition, regardless of the score and the accolades?* The answer was "Yes!" So I decided to recommit myself to being a gymnast, and this time, to throw myself into the sport, not just to win competitions, but for the art of it, and the love of it.

I also wanted to ground myself in the things I loved in my life *outside* of gymnastics: being with my family, hanging out with friends, laughing and telling jokes. I needed to get away from attaching my self-worth to the roller-coaster of performance and scores.

But without the intense drive to win, my performance suffered. At the 2007 US Nationals, held nine months before the 2008 Olympic team was selected, I bombed. My performance was rocky and for the first time in nine years, I didn't even make the national team. There I was, a previous two-time World Championship team member and 2004 Olympic alternate, not even on the radar for the team selection process. I had to own up to the truth: what I was doing wasn't working.

The night I returned home from the Nationals, I spent hours looking myself in the eyes in the mirror, as tears streamed down my face. I was harboring a lot of pain and a lot of guilt. Underneath it all, I was still angry, still wondering why things hadn't worked out my way in 2004. I was ready to pack it in. I remember talking to some friends around that time and saying, "Maybe I'm just too old. Maybe I should just retire."

A few days later, a friend of mine, a 2000 Olympian himself, handed me a book, and said, "You need to read this." I took it from him and saw on the cover a picture of a white-haired guy with a big smile, and the words: How to Get from Where You Are to Where You Want to Be. I thought, *No book can help me get where I want to be; my problem is different*. But when my coach recommended the same book, I decided to give it a chance.

The book was *The Success Principles*, and one of the first things the author, Jack Canfield, says is that, to be successful, you have to take 100% responsibility for everything that happens in your life. That was a tough one to swallow. I was sure that life had played against me, and that if I could just figure out what had really gone down, I could make it right.

But now I saw that beating that very dead horse had gotten me exactly nowhere. Whatever had happened was done, and harboring all that anger was useless. For me, committing to take 100% responsibility meant turning all that "looking for someone to blame" energy inward and starting to analyze how my brain worked. Where was my fear was coming from, and what was causing the negative loop of thoughts in my head?

In *The Success Principles*, Jack writes that even the most successful people have to deal with fear and negativity on a daily basis, and yet they still choose to go forward toward their goals. Man! That really hit home for me. I'd thought that struggling with those things meant I was broken. Now I didn't feel so isolated and alone. Negative thoughts, rejection, fear—they're just part of the process. But now they became challenges for me to overcome, rather than huge roadblocks and evidence of my failure.

My coach said it was like I had flipped a switch; he could see the light go on in me. The next week in the gym, working with him on my training plans, I recommitted to my dream of being an Olympian, and from that point on, I spent 24 hours a day devoted to this goal. But the goal had expanded: I wanted to be an Olympian in *life*.

Following another piece of Jack's advice about the power of visualization, I made a huge vision board and a mind map and put them up on my bedroom wall. They were the first things I saw when I walked into the room. Every day after practice I looked at them and said, "Yep. Yep. Doing that. Doing that. Doing that." They helped me break down my huge, lofty, overwhelming Olympic goal into areas of daily focus that I could manage.

Inspired by Jack's book, I harnessed the energy of my subconscious mind using affirmations. Every night before I went to bed,

I wrote *"I am on the 2008 Olympic Team. I am on the 2008 Olympic Team,"* over and over and over, filling up over 100 notebook pages, front and back.

Before long, *The Success Principles* became the "working bible" of our gym. The coaches routinely referenced the principles, and my team-mates and I used them to inspire each other. It became an energy you could feel within our gym.

I made it to the 2008 Olympic tryouts in Philly, and sailed right through. I felt happy and clear and on top of my game. When they called ten of the gymnasts competing for the remaining two spots on the Olympic team into the board room, I was very, very confident. I'd nailed all my routines. I had done all this work on my life. Hey, I'd read *The Success Principles* and put them into practice! I thought, *For sure, they're gonna name me to the team this time.*

They read off the names of the two team members. I didn't hear my name. *What?!* I threw my hands up into the air. It was a gesture of absolute bewilderment about life and the universe and its workings. In a cruel repeat of 2004, I heard the words, "Raj Bhavsar, alternate."

As I left the room, a reporter from NBC stuck a mike in my face and asked me how I felt about being named an alternate a second time. I answered with one sentence, "There is no extrinsic event that can defeat my sense of inner accomplishment." After stumbling half-there through a few more interviews, I left the facility and flew back to Houston.

Sitting on the plane, I took stock of the situation. I wasn't mad the way I'd been before. When you take 100% responsibility for your life, anger and frustration just don't stick around that long. Plus, I had developed the philosophy that gymnastics was just one piece of me, not my entire being, so if I didn't get this I was still going to be okay. Still, I was honestly baffled and taken aback that after all I had done, I hadn't made the team again.

At home, I set my bags down inside my apartment and took a walk. There was a long colonnade of trees on both sides of the street, making a canopy of branches above me. I remember stopping at one point and looking up through a small opening in the trees to the night sky. I stood there, staring up at the stars. There was no anger. I wasn't asking "Why?" Instead, I felt a sense of peace and connection with the universe.

And although part of me was ready to put out the fire in my heart to be an Olympian, in that moment something in me said "Keep the dream alive. There's no way this is over." I was proud of my training and my performance, and I refused to extinguish my flame. The next morning, I called the USA gymnastics officials and told them I'd be honored to be an alternate.

For the next week, I trained hard and stayed ready. Then it was announced that Paul Hamm, the 2004 gold medalist and now on the Olympic team for 2008, had made the decision to withdraw from the US Olympic team due to injuries. One of the three alternates would be chosen to replace him. The committee would decide which one of us it would be within 24 hours.

It was probably the most excruciating, yet exciting, 24 hours of my entire life. My dad was out of town and my mom was helping me pack for Beijing. I kept thinking that I should go get my pen and paper and write my affirmation a gazillion more times. But I was just too busy. That night, when I finally had the time, I picked up the pen and sat for a minute looking at the sheet of paper in front of me. I knew I had done everything that could be done. Instead of my affirmation, I wrote, *LET THE DREAM CHASE YOU* in large letters across the page, underlined it, and went to bed.

The next day was decision day. At the gym, my coach, my sports performance counselor, and I got on the phone with the USA Gymnastics PR person, who started the call by reviewing Paul's situation. Then the president of USA Gymnastics came on the line to give the official announcement. He went into his whole spiel, saying, we're very happy about this decision, and on and on. Inside I'm begging him, *Say the name! Just say the name! Please, is it me or not?!*

Finally he said, "So at this time we'd like to announce the new member of the 2008 Olympic team . . . Raj Bhavsar."

With a shout, I fell to my knees. Then, smiling and crying at the same time, I stood up and hugged my coach. I hugged my counselor. I hugged everyone. I was ecstatic and inside I thought, *See?! I knew it!* I'd done everything I could to deserve it and now, I finally had it. And for that I was grateful to the universe. I was grateful to God. And I was grateful to Paul Hamm; it was a tough but honorable decision to have made.

For me, it was a dream come true—and the start of a new mission. After my celebration in the office, I quickly began focusing on the job ahead. It was going to be a challenge because we were primarily a team of rookies.

Then when we got to Beijing, Paul's brother Morgan Hamm was also injured and had to be replaced, so now we were a brand new team, not a single one of us had any Olympic experience. The entire media and even people in the gymnastics community had written us off.

I remember being in the Olympic village the night before the competition, sitting with the whole team and reading the press about us in the Internet room. There were many commentators who thought we might not even make it into team finals.

That was when I committed to doing whatever I could to help keep our outlook positive. We weren't going to let someone else's opinion affect our performance. After reading all the doom and gloom from the press, the six of us all went out onto the balcony and had a meeting. We talked about caring for each other as human beings first, and as athletes, second, and about having each other's backs no matter what happened. The road we were about to take was ours to cherish forever, win or lose. It was the most grounding, humbling talk I've ever had with teammates. It gave us the confidence to walk onto the competition floor as a team, first and foremost, with our heads held high, regardless of the result.

The next day we went out there and had the meet of our lives. With the entire arena chanting. "U.S.A. U.S.A." we edged out the Germans and in an incredible upset, won a bronze medal! It was the most wonderful feeling imaginable—we were so proud of ourselves, of each other, and of our country. I went home and pinned my medal to my vision board, where it is to this day.

The greatest thing I got from those years isn't the title of being an Olympian, and it certainly isn't the medal. It's that I now have a formula for getting the results I want in life: once I find a passion, it's a matter of latching on to that dream with complete conviction and unwavering tenacity. And then, when I've gone as far as I can, I trust the universe . . . and let the dream chase me!

A BLIND MAN'S VISION

Charlie Collins

My parents and I sat in the doctor's office as he gave us the diagnosis. "I'm afraid it's juvenile macular degeneration," he said, his tone grave. "There's nothing we can do to save Charlie's sight." I was nine years old.

At 13, I received a certificate from the state of Connecticut declaring that I was legally blind. I didn't need the certificate to know that—for the last three years, the writing on the chalkboard had progressively disappeared, and in the school hallways, the faces of the people I passed had become dim and gray. Although I could still make out shapes, colors, and areas of light and dark, my world seemed to be shrinking rapidly around me. The certificate only cemented the belief growing inside that I was going to fail in life, and my self-esteem began its long nose-dive.

I struggled through high school—seemingly on an all-out quest to prove that my negative self-image was accurate. I tried to numb my pain by drinking and even taking drugs, but that never solved anything for long and only ended up creating more problems in my life. When I graduated, I tried college twice, but flunked out both times. After that, I moved back in with my parents and began working odd jobs, landscaping, and grooming ski trails and tennis courts.

As a kid, I'd wanted to fly planes, be a cop or a private detective, do something with engines, and go *fast!* But all those ambitions had died with my diagnosis. After high school and my failed attempts at college, I literally had no dreams, sure that my life, dominated by my disability, was going nowhere.

One day, when I was about 24, I was on a landscaping job, cutting the grass at a local motorcycle dealership. I had just finished edging the walk and I stood up for a moment, aware of the long line of shining new motorcycles parked in front of me.

Motorcycles were special to me. Even though I couldn't hold a driver's license, I owned a dirt bike which I often took out in the woods behind my house where I had walked a trail and memorized it. Some of my happiest moments of that period were spent speeding along through the trees, the breeze ruffling my hair. At those times, I didn't feel quite so blind.

Standing in front of the parked motorcycles, I fell into a daydream, imagining myself racing, leaning into corners, the roar of the engine filling my ears. Suddenly, I felt a tap on my shoulder. Startled, I turned around to see a bearded ZZ Top-looking guy. I recognized him immediately: it was Jimbo, the owner of the dealership. I often came in to buy parts for my dirt bike and we knew each other by name. Assuming he didn't like the job I'd done on the lawn, I cringed inside, waiting for the dressing-down I expected.

"Charlie," he said, "I was wondering if you'd like to work for me."

My first thought was, *Why would he ask a dumb blind guy?* But all I said was, "To do what?"

"Well, I know you love motorcycles, and I think you'd make a good salesman."

I was stunned. I told Jimbo I'd think it over.

That night I lay in the same single bed I'd slept in my whole life—the bed where I'd spent so many nights crying or wondering why I existed or even thinking "Boy, wouldn't it be nice not to wake up tomorrow." But tonight I was arguing with myself. I truly believed I wasn't good enough for the job. Yet, I really wanted to try. Torn between fear and hope, I cried out inside, "If there's a God up there, I really could use some help here. There's a big part of me that would love that job. Please remove whatever is blocking me from saying "Yes" and just giving this a shot. I can't allow this blindness to control me anymore! I can't allow a disease in my eyes to take over my entire thought process, my body, every inch of me—to let it kill me! Please, help me." After tossing and turning for hours, I eventually fell asleep.

In the morning, I went straight to the dealership and told Jimbo I'd take the job. "But," I said, "do you have any idea how poor my eyesight is?"

Jimbo said he knew there was something going on with my eyes, but it didn't matter to him. "I don't know you as a guy with an eye condition; I know you as a guy who's passionate and enthusiastic, and who loves this type of stuff!"

"Really?" I said. "What the heck; I never saw that."

Jimbo gave me a chance, and I wasn't going to let him down. I threw myself into my new job and discovered that I was really good at sales. To my amazement, within two years, I had worked myself up the ladder and become the co-owner of the dealership—a $2-million-a-year business! This was beyond my conception of anything I could have even imagined for myself. During those years, I also married a lovely woman I'd known since sixth grade, and bought my first house. Wow, there I was, living the American dream!

Yet strangely enough, I still wasn't happy. I had the toys, the prestige, the power, and the money, but something was missing—something I vaguely recognized as a sense of purpose and meaning in my life. On top of that, I had started trying to hide my eye disease from my customers, and this pretense and self-inflicted pressure to be "normal" was getting to me.

So I sold my share of the dealership and took a year off to figure out what to do next. During that year I realized that, even with my success, I still felt unworthy. My self-esteem had been temporarily propped up by my business accomplishments, but underneath, at my core, I still considered myself that "dumb blind guy."

As I mulled over my career options, I promised myself that whatever I picked would have to help me find a sense of purpose in my life, and most of all, allow me to be myself—vision impairment and all. Once I got that clear, bingo! That was it! I had the idea to start a company to help other people with vision impairments. So I founded Vision Dynamics, a company that supplies products and services to people living with low vision and blindness so that they can lead independent and happy lives.

What I still didn't know was that vision impairment has less to do with the eyes and more to do with the brain and our thoughts.

That knowledge came a few years later, when I began to look into the world of personal development. I'd heard of it, but didn't really know much about it. One day, I Googled "self-esteem" and found a website for Jack Canfield. This guy sold audio books. Perfect! I bought one called *Maximum Confidence* and began listening. I was so excited by what I heard that halfway through the first CD, I paused the disc to run to my computer and buy more of his audio books: *The Aladdin Factor* and *The Power of Focus*. I was blown away! This guy knew exactly what was going on with me—down to the specific wording of the negative self-talk that still ran constantly through my mind.

Best of all, Jack had *answers*. I began using his tools and techniques, practicing what I was learning from his CDs, both at work and at home. Soon I started teaching my staff a few of Jack's tools. "Today, we're going to practice visualization," I said to them. "Isn't it cool that blind people can visualize?" Of course, I'd been visualizing all my life, but I didn't know that's what I was doing. Most of my visualizations were negative, focusing on lack, scarcity, and what I felt I couldn't have. Slowly, I began turning that around.

For the next two years, I listened to Jack's tapes over and over, and things in my life got better and better. I was really impressed with this Jack Canfield guy. So impressed that in early 2008, I found myself sitting in the first row at a three-day Jack Canfield seminar, hearing the man speak live.

Just getting to the seminar had been a huge stretch for me. I'd traveled across the country to California alone—something I didn't know if I could pull off. I'd retrieved my luggage, found transportation to the hotel, and navigated through a completely unfamiliar building by myself. I was practicing trust, practicing "I can!" Whenever I started telling myself, "You can't," I'd quickly change it to "You can! Remember that Jack says you can."

A few weeks earlier, when I'd registered for the program, I hadn't told anyone I was vision-impaired. Now, surrounded by more than 300 smart, successful people, I tried to hide my disability. I thought these people might feel sorry for me or look down on me.

It wasn't a problem the first day. It was great to hear Jack in person and observe how he worked with people on the course. I hung on every word. I took copious notes, writing with a big black Sharpie—the only way I could see what I was writing—until the lady to my right asked me to please use a different pen because the fumes from the Sharpie were bothering her. I didn't want to tell her why I needed to use that particular type of pen, so I took out a ball point pen and pretended to use it.

The next day, the hiding thing came to a head. I arrived for the morning meeting and saw our name badges laid out on a table outside the door. I couldn't see the writing on them at all. I looked around to make sure no one was watching me and then bent down with my nose an inch from the badges, trying to find mine and straightening up whenever I heard someone approach—which was every 30 seconds or so.

After a few minutes of this, I was panicked, ready to run back to my hotel room, skip the meeting, and hide until it was time for my flight back to Connecticut.

The doors were about to close when I had an idea. The next person who walked up to the table was a woman. "Excuse me," I said. "I left my glasses in my room. My name's Charlie. Can you point out my badge to me?" She smiled and handed it to me. I thanked her, my heart pounding, and sprinted into the meeting room.

At the first break, I walked up to the stage and introduced myself to Jack. We began talking and for some reason, I told him about my experience with the name badges. After the break, I sat down in my chair, ready for more, when I heard Jack say, "Somebody please give Charlie the microphone." Then he asked me to stand up.

"Hi, Charlie," Jack said. "I want you to stand up and face the people in the room. Now, tell them what you told me at the break."

I was mad! How could he expose me like that! How could he make me tell everyone my secret? But I did it. And as I spoke, I could feel more and more power flowing inside me. And at the end of my story, people clapped!

Jack said to me, "So, Charlie, I think you get it: you need to stop living your life this way. As of right now, you're no longer going to allow that legal blindness to run your life." Then he looked around the room and asked, "Is there anybody here who would say no if Charlie approached them and asked for help?"

The room went nuts. Everyone was calling out, "I'd help him!" "I'd love to help!" "Of course I'd help him!"

Jack continued, "Human beings *like* to help each other. That's what we're here for, to serve and help each other—and all of us need help at certain times. Now, do you believe that, Charlie?"

To my surprise, I did.

For the rest of the seminar, I had a great time. I felt somewhat vulnerable—and yet more open, authentic, and empowered than I'd ever felt before. And because I had felt so much growth working with Jack in person, before I left that 3-day seminar I signed up for every damn course he taught. The next one I went to—Breakthrough to Success, Jack's week-long training program—was also a life-changing experience. It was there that I finally discovered my true calling: being an inspirational transformational speaker.

Today, I have two careers that I'm passionate about. After selling Vision Dynamics I joined Optelec US, the largest worldwide provider and manufacturer of low vision and blindness products, as their Chief Marketing Officer. I'm also the internal corporate trainer, and in this role I conduct success principle trainings which have helped shape a winning culture and a much more productive team.

And I'm also a professional speaker. Through my company Charlie Collins International, The MaximEyes Advantage, I travel around the country speaking to groups of people, both sighted and blind, about how we can overcome our blind spots—because no matter how good a person's eyesight is, we all have them!

In fact, one of the most important things I learned from Jack is that we all lose our vision when we block ourselves with negative thinking patterns. Even people with perfect eyesight can't see their way to creating a happy life for themselves until they put their thoughts to work *for* them, instead of against them.

And after becoming a Canfield Certified Trainer, I'm also conducting seminars on the success principles.

Today, I am living my true life purpose and it's a great one: I teach people how to "see" again.

KICKING BURNOUT IN THE "ASH"

Stéphane Fournier

In the ten years since I'd started my career, I had only cried twice at work.

Ten intense years as a corporate lawyer. Multi-billion-dollar deals. Crazy deadlines. Last-minute head-spinning issues. The works.

Yet the only thing that had brought me to tears those two times at the office was receiving the news of a grandparent's passing.

I took pride in that dry-spell track record. I really did.

Machismo incarnate.

Then came the crash of August 17th, 2010. My professional crash, that is.

A year earlier, I had become one of the youngest directors ever appointed within the department of the Canadian government that monitors the country's financial institutions. But as the leader of one the department's most dynamic legislative units, my ego got in the way.

I considered what I did an art, and saw myself as a modern-day Da Vinci, churning out one work of genius after another. Night, day, weekday or weekend—it didn't matter. I was on an unfettered "Never Say No" crusade (NSN for short), fueled by adrenaline and a burning desire to prove that I could do it all, all the time, and with all-out quality.

The day I crashed, my body and mind had had enough. The web I had so meticulously woven to "keep it together" came undone, and I melted down in front of my colleagues and sobbed in a way I'd rarely done in my life. Within a day, I knew in my gut I had to stop working, but I couldn't accept it. I had to come to grips with it the following week when my physician looked me in the eye and confirmed it: Burn-out, requiring an indefinite medical leave from work.

The first weeks of my leave were rough. The adrenaline had subsided, and I had trouble both sleeping and getting out of bed. A bad combination. Plus, I didn't want to see or speak to anyone. My wife reached out to me, but I didn't want to talk. A few of my colleagues called me, but I didn't answer or return their calls.

The way I saw it, I was a workplace victim. My colleagues should have seen this coming. *They* totally understood my NSN M.O. *They* knew I wouldn't allow myself to say no. It was up to *them* to short-circuit NSN by not asking me to take on something *they* should have realized would bring me to the edge. Yet they were still at work and I was stuck at home, feeling lost and humiliated.

One morning, about one month into my leave, my six-year-old son said to me, "Papa, tomorrow is the Terry Fox Run. You've *got* to come!"

The Terry Fox Run is a huge marathon in Canada that has taken place every September since 1980. That year, after having his right leg amputated because of bone cancer, the 21-year-old Terry Fox embarked on an improbable journey he called the Marathon of Hope. A run across Canada, from the east coast to the west, to raise money for the fight against cancer and as a testament to the power of the human spirit. Fox, however, was forced to end his run after 143 days and 3,339 miles. When he recognized he wouldn't be able to reach the Pacific, he bequeathed his mission to others. Thus, the Terry Fox Run was born.

Although I had always regarded the Run—which raises millions of dollars every year for cancer research—as an important event, with all I'd been through, I wasn't up to it. I opened my mouth to say no, but looking into my son's expectant eyes, I couldn't do it. I nodded, forcing a smile. I would go.

I managed to get my body to the Run that September morning, but I felt hollow and depressed. Children, parents, grandparents, and friends were smiling and cheering around me at the starting line, but little of that sunk in.

My ears perked up, though, at the sound of the conversation between two women behind me. ". . . So it's a great book by one of the *Chicken Soup for the Soul* guys," I overheard one say to the other. "He teaches you to take100% responsibility for your life . . ."

That was it. No title or author's name. The sound of the rest of the conversation was drowned out by the rising roar of the crowd. Just *Chicken Soup* and taking 100% responsibility for your life.

I didn't give those words any more thought until the November day, two months later, when my son blasted through the front door after my wife, my daughter, and he returned from the video store. "Papa! Papa!" he shouted as he kicked his galoshes off his feet, the snow flying everywhere. "Look what I have!" It was *Into the Wind*, a documentary about Terry Fox.

As my kids and I sat side-by-side on the couch, watching the documentary, the words I had overheard at the Run came back to me: "Take 100% responsibility for your life . . . ."

Suddenly, it hit me. *Wow!* I thought. Terry had been an otherwise ordinary young man with a passion for sports, who lost one of his legs due to the ravages of bone cancer. This otherwise ordinary young man had become extraordinary *because* he saw opportunity in an incredibly difficult event. The opportunity to raise awareness about cancer and funds to end it. The opportunity to show the power of human will. And the opportunity to change attitudes toward people with disabilities.

Terry's story. That has to be the meaning of taking responsibility for your life!

My heart pounded. My mind raced. *I need a copy of that "responsibility" book. Pronto.*

Within a few minutes, Google handed me the name and the title of the book. *Yes!* Within a few hours, I was sitting on that same couch, staring at a paperback copy of Jack Canfield's *The Success Principles*.

Opening the book, I began to read. The first chapter hit me like a blow to the chest. To say that Principle 1, *Take 100% Responsibility for Your Life*, prompted me to face the reality of my situation is to put it, well, mildly. The essence of Principle 1 is that events can and do influence your life; but at the end of the day, it's your responses to those events that determine your outcomes.

Jack uses an equation to make this clear: Event + Response = Outcome. He then crystallizes the concept in a single sentence: "In short, you thought the thoughts, you created the feelings, you made the choice, you said the words, and that's why you are where you are now."

Oh man, was I gasping for air after I read that! I thought, *Uh-oh. My colleagues weren't responsible for my burnout. It was my own doing, my own NSN attitude that did me in.* Through my own choices, I had created, or had allowed to be created, the conditions that had led to my medical leave. That was a bitter pill to swallow.

Instead of being inspired, I felt worse. Fortunately, I thought about Terry Fox the next morning and how he saw opportunities in his cancer—something even harder to swallow. So I decided to reread Principle 1 with a fresh perspective, lingering over the Event + Response = Outcome equation.

And that's when the "Hell, yeah!" moment came.

My burnout was an outcome. No doubt about that.

But it was also an event! And the outcome of that event depended on my response to it—right now.

What if I gave my burnout an empowering meaning like Terry Fox did with his cancer? I asked myself. *What kind of outcomes could I generate with that response?*

That was it. The turning point. At that moment, I reframed my burnout in terms of opportunity.

An opportunity to reconnect with myself, including my health.

An opportunity to reconnect with my family.

An opportunity to witness the compassion of my colleagues.

An opportunity to learn how to work more effectively and resiliently.

An opportunity to show that not only can I bounce back from burnout, but also be better than ever because of it.

And did I ever seize those opportunities.

That morning, I started cycling again. Nirvana. And in the process, I rekindled my passion for a sport that I've realized is my version of mediation on wheels.

That day I was more present with my wife and children, deliberately creating moments filled with understanding and expressions of love.

I then reached out to my colleagues who had reached out to me. I filled my calendar with coffee and lunch dates—in my case, a healthy step towards my eventual transition back into the workplace.

That night, I experienced the best sleep in a very long time. Finally, there was a point to it all and I was clearly on the mend. My mind was at ease.

A few days later, I reached out to my workplace's employee wellness services, which led to some great coaching. The result? I was back at the office within a few months, fully equipped with powerful tools and perspectives on work—and myself.

More than a year has passed since I returned to work, and it's 5:00 a.m. as I type these words. Aliveness is pumping loud and proud in my veins after seven hours of sound sleep. It's winter in Ottawa now, so I am about to hit the stationary bike for 30 minutes, as I usually do at this time of the day. Before the bike, though, I write. Everything from expressions of gratitude and personal stories (like this one), to letters to my kids and lines for my upcoming book. This is the time for myself. Writing and exercising in the morning are now part of my "optimal outcomes protocol" before I go out into the world, so I can be at my sustainable best.

My wife and kids are still asleep, but they'll be up soon. Before I leave for work, I will hug each of them, tightly, and whisper softly into their ear: "I love you. With all my heart. Thank you for blessing my life."

And how are things at work? I have a new position now, one that better suits my passion for research and writing. My relationships with my colleagues are great, and we keep the lines of communication open about workloads.

NSN is a thing of the past. My new approach to work: be a response-able team player, one who exercises his ability to respond to a request or other event in the way he feels is best, depending on the outcome he wishes to produce.

It's still a high-octane environment, as any work environment can be. And that's okay. Because I know now that no else but me holds—and strikes—the match. And it all started with Jack's Success Principle 1: taking 100% responsibility for my life.

YO ROMEO!

Romeo Marquez Jr.

As a kid, I was always the life of the party. I'd put on Michael Jackson and dance, dance, dance! Even when I was just five or six years old, visiting San Francisco with my parents or grandparents, I'd see people break dancing in the streets, and I'd dance right over to them. I had this itch for movement and entertaining. My grandpa saw that in me and played as my wingman, my best friend. We'd go on walks, play cards, or he'd show me magic tricks. He (and my dad) could always make me laugh. I get my wit and humor from them *and* learned how to make other people laugh.

In high school, I got more into sports, because it was considered a cooler thing to do than performing. I wanted to keep my cool kid image, so I held that bug inside me. Around this same time my grandpa was in and out of the hospital, and one day he passed away. That was the first time I'd lost somebody in my life, and I thought the world was over. My role model and one of the people I expressed myself most freely with was gone. I put up a wall around myself and only told a few friends about my grandpa dying. I didn't feel like most people I knew would understand.

When I started community college, my older sister could see I was struggling and was worried about me; she was afraid I'd make some wrong decisions. She gave me a calendar with inspirational quotes that she hoped would spark new possibilities in me.

And they did. Reading the quotes lifted my spirits and made me see that it was okay to be myself, even okay to fail. My dad wanted me to be an electrical engineer, but instead I signed up for my first acting class. I didn't know what it would be like. But in the class I noticed how people responded to me, and one of my teachers said I should audition for a part in a play. "You won't know if you don't go," she said, and that stuck with me.

I was scared, but I followed my teacher's advice to make bold choices. In the audition, the director was looking for someone charismatic and outgoing. I used my talent for back flips in a contained "wild and crazy" style during my monologue, and I got the part. Other roles and even some awards followed. Finally, I had my old self back again: expressing myself freely, having fun—and dancing like Michael Jackson!

I transferred to UCLA and graduated with a B.A. in acting. I knew I wanted to be an actor, but I also knew that an actor's lifestyle is up and down, constant auditions, and a roller coaster of unknowing. Was there a way to be an actor and take more control of my life?

My sister gave me self-help book after self-help book to read to help me figure out where I was going with my life. I liked those books. It got so that whenever I was in a bookstore, I went straight to the personal development section. One day I saw *The Success Principles* by Jack Canfield on a shelf. The book seemed to say to me, "Hey Romeo, come on over here." The book was thick, kind of intimidating, but the subtitle attracted me—"How to Get from Where You Are to Where You Want to Be." Once I started reading the introduction, I knew I would buy the book. At home, I immersed myself in it. I highlighted pages, wrote all over it. I've read that book so many times that the cover fell off.

Reading Jack's words felt like a dad talking to me. He taught me to open my mind to all possibilities and to welcome risks. Some of the ideas in Jack's book I'd read before, like taking 100% responsibility for our lives. But I'd always set those books (and the exercises in them) aside, thinking, *I'll do it later, I'll do it later*. But Jack broke things down in a simple way that made me want to do everything *right now*.

Because I was focusing on building an acting career, auditioning, and teaching acting, the story in the book about Jim Carrey's experience with visualization and goal-setting fascinated me. In 1990, before Jim was famous, he used to drive his old car up

Mulholland Drive and say to himself, "Directors want to work with me; I'm going to be a successful actor." He even wrote himself a ten-million dollar check "for acting services rendered" and dated it for Thanksgiving, 1995. He carried that check around in his wallet for years. The crazy thing is, it worked—by 1995 he was making $20 million per picture. He got what he wanted.

One of the exercises in *The Success Principles* involves writing a list of one hundred and one goals. For one of mine, I said I wanted to meet and work with Jim Carrey. Day after day, I held that idea in my mind, really picturing myself working with Jim Carrey. A week or two after that, I got a call to be an extra on Jim Carrey's movie, "The Number 23." I thought, *Okay! How cool is that?*

Working as an extra, you're in the background, and you don't communicate with the actors or the directors—new actors do this as part of the process for getting into the Screen Actors Guild. In one scene, I was a college student sitting in a classroom. After five or ten minutes, one of the assistant directors told everyone to get off the set so they could make some changes. A lot of the actors went to the food services room where they had snacks and drinks. We were all talking, asking each other, "Where are you from?" "How long have you been acting?" "Who's your agent?" when Jim Carrey walked through the door. Everybody was poking everyone else and whispering, ""It's him. It's Jim Carrey." I was trying to keep my cool, but thinking, *Oh my gosh! It's Jim Carrey! Whoa! This stuff works!*

Jim walked over to the buffet table and was getting some tea, but nobody approached him. We weren't supposed to. A few minutes later, the assistant director called us back to the set. Everyone left except for Jim and me.

This was my chance. I went right up to him and said, "Hi, I'm Romeo."

He said, "Hi, I'm Jim," and I said, "I know."

Then I told him I'd just read a story about him and visualization, and could he please tell me a bit more about that. He said, "You know what, Romeo? It works. I tell people that if it can work for me, it can work for anybody."

I told him I read about the $10 million check, and that I did the same thing for myself.

He said, "Really?" He felt good that his story had inspired me.

After that, whenever we had a break on set, Jim and I would talk about the Super Bowl or something, just joking around. It was fun to be on a first-name basis with one of my heroes. But more than that, it was exciting to know first-hand that visualization really does work.

I had friends who toured as actors, and so I made that my next goal. Soon I had the chance to do just that, working in an educational theater program for kids all over California that focused on violence prevention and intelligent decision-making. I was getting paid as a touring actor, and also teaching and having an impact on the younger generation. Two of the things that are most important to me. Still, after doing that for a while, I thought, *I like what I'm doing, but I know my talent and words can have an even bigger impact. I want to do this nationally.* It was time for a new goal.

Jack says to be very specific with your goals, so I looked around and found a position that was exactly what I wanted to do. I set my sights on working as a trainer with an organization called Challenge Day, which is recognized internationally as being one of the top programs for celebrating students and inspiring them to find their place in the world. I went full throttle—goal setting, visualization, affirmations—applying all the stuff I learned from Jack to getting this new position. I auditioned and was accepted! I went through an intensive six-month training, then was selected to be one of five new leaders to present programs in high schools all over North America. Success!

I also wrote an inspirational one-man show and have performed it in New York, San Francisco, Las Vegas, and Colorado.

This work on a national level has taken me to the global level: a few years ago, I gave my first TEDx talk in Chennai, India. And from that TEDx opportunity I've received an invitation to return to India—this time to do a speaking tour—as well as to do trainings in Europe. And this is just the beginning . . .

All this came from a few simple seeds that Jack Canfield

planted: What you want is possible. Take action now. Don't wait for opportunities—create them.

Now, in between all my travels, I visit my community college from time to time, speaking to the same acting class that I first took. I remind the students that anything is possible and that it's okay to fail—they just have to get right back up and keep going. "What's important is that you go *big*. Everything you want in life is just outside your comfort zone." Then I say, "Hey, do you want to hear a story about Jim Carrey?"

THE MAN WITH THE MIDAS TOUCH

John Calub

In 2005, I was on top of the world. A few years earlier, I'd spearheaded the launch of a hip new restaurant in Manila, where I lived, and it had taken off. With some partners, I'd expanded and business at the *three* restaurants we co-owned was booming. I was a Manila success story!

And then it happened. Our revenues began to dip and quarrels between my partners and I erupted. One by one the restaurants shut down. And I lost my money—all of it.

I don't know which was more painful: losing my money or losing face with the people I loved the most. My family couldn't accept the change in my fate. Neither could my girlfriend. She left me for another man.

The downward spiral continued. I moved in with my parents, and to make matters worse, I was borrowing money left and right, not only from my immediate family, but from *all* of my relatives. Soon, they all began avoiding me. No one would take my calls or respond to any of my text messages. Broke and miserable, I locked myself in my room, I didn't want to see or talk to anyone.

Then one day after about eight months of this despair, I'd had enough. I did the only thing I could think of. I prayed. "God, please help me get out of my misery." He must have heard me. Maybe I heard myself. Or both. On that very day, I made the decision not to be poor any more. I vowed to make it big—really big.

There's a saying that the universe rewards action. Just 24 hours after vowing to change my life—after saying, "This will end today," an old client of mine, who I met while selling advertising, called me. He had learned about my misfortune and, though I hadn't ever written professionally, he offered to take me on as a writer for the biggest newspaper in the Philippines. My assignment would be to interview successful people and write a column about their success stories and the principles they live by.

After being an entrepreneur for years, it was a hard decision to go back to a job. But I swallowed the bitter pill. Little did I know it was the answer to my prayer.

My very first assignment was to interview Jack Canfield, who was coming to Manila to give a seminar. A few days later, I met with Jack at a book signing, where I was also given a free ticket to attend the next day's seminar. In exchange, I would write a feature article for my paper about Jack and his work.

Sitting in the seminar, with my arms crossed tightly across my chest, I listened carefully as Jack described his principles for success. At first I was very skeptical. He had crazy ideas, like cutting out pictures and putting them on a board, and looking at it every day, and then *feeling* as though you already had what you wanted. My rational mind said, *Yeah, right. Like looking at some pictures is going to help me get what I want.* What a joke.

At one point, he talked about Dr. Masaru Emoto's famous experiment with water crystals and showed pictures of how water can be affected by our thoughts, words, and feelings. Though I was intrigued, I still wasn't convinced.

After the seminar, I went home and thought about what Jack had shared that day. My mind was filled with so many doubts and questions, but then it dawned on me: Jack was a very, very successful guy who had used these concepts, and here I was totally broke. Who would you listen to? Besides, I had nothing to lose. I had already lost everything! I decided to follow his advice and see what happened.

Jack had autographed a copy of *The Success Principles* for me, and I started reading it. Every week I worked with a different principle. I began using visualization and even created one of those "crazy" dream boards I'd been so skeptical about.

The first image I cut out to put on the board was a picture of a BMW—my dream car. At the time, I was far away from that. To get around, I was either walking or riding in a Jeepney, a very crowded mode of public transportation here in the Philippines. But my doubt had turned to trust. And it worked! Within a year, I bought my first BMW.

Another important thing I discovered in Jack's seminar was the principle of passion. When I was younger, I worked at so many jobs. I even sold janitorial services. But I was doing that just to make a living, to pay my bills. During the seminar, Jack led us through The Passion Test, and I became aware of my love of teaching. I truly feel it's my gift and purpose. So the breakthrough goal that I created at that seminar was not just to become a motivational speaker and a coach, but to become the Philippines' #1 Success Coach.

I started by launching a series of seminars on success, teaching the principles I learned from Jack. Then I went into coaching and began consulting for different companies. My income began rising quickly, and soon I was earning over a million pesos. In the Philippines, a million pesos is a lot of money! Next, I combined my passion for traveling with my passion for teaching and began traveling around the world.

Once I was at an expo in Los Angeles and a woman, who I later found out is a celebrity psychic there, came up to me and said, "I feel that you're somebody who is a magnet for money, and everything you touch turns to gold." I was a surprised by her comment, but it must have stuck in my consciousness. I began wearing gold on stage. I bought gold Doc Martens and a gold coat. Even my BMW is gold. And it's certainly led to gold . . .

Today, my training company is the biggest profit center of all of my companies. I know it's successful because I'm doing what I'm passionate about. Before, I hadn't been doing what I loved, and so my success was hit-and-miss. Now I'm so enthusiastic about teaching the success principles that people flock to see me—I've even earned seven-figures in one day!

Sadly, my relationship with my family was much slower to turn around. They were wary of me, and my seminars. Think about it:

a broke guy telling people how to be successful. In the Philippines most people live by the principle of "To See is to Believe."

I knew that cleaning up my messes was going to be important to win back my family's confidence. Over time, I did whatever I could to clear out my negative past, and I repaid all of my debts.

Buying the new BMW certainly got their attention. Still, it was going to take more than that to make my parents believers in what I was doing. They had to see for themselves what I was up to, so I came up with a plan. One night, I invited them to dinner and asked them to pick me up at the hotel where I was giving a seminar. Only they didn't know I was giving it.

When they got to the hotel, they were directed to my event. There were hundreds of people in the room when I looked up and saw them sit down. Now they had no choice but to listen, and they were shocked—shocked to see so many people attending my seminars. Shocked to see that I was transforming those people's lives.

Things changed between us after that night. In fact, though I'm grateful for my financial success, perhaps my biggest success is my wonderful relationship with my family, especially my immediate family. I now hug and say I love you to my parents—without reservation. I know a lot of parents have ideas about what they want their children to do or be, and it's doesn't necessarily match an individual's dreams. I'm lucky. My parents support me 100% and even attend my seminars whenever they can. My dad is my number one fan! And because of my financial success, I'm able to spend more time with them, not something that I was able to do when I was working jobs just to make a living.

Jack has helped me see that you can really have it all. My first dream board was created in 2006, and since then I've achieved about 70% of what I set out to achieve, including training with the world's best mentors including Brian Tracy, Tony Buzan, T. Harv Eker, Anthony Robbins, Tolly Burkan (Mentor of Tony Robbins and Founder of The Global Firewalking Movement), Jay Conrad Levinson, Robert Kiyosaki co-author of Rich Dad, Poor Dad, and Donald Trump. The best part—I also attracted the opportunity to have lunch or dinner with each one of them!

Because of the Success Principles, I'm the highest paid motivational speaker in the country and well on my way to becoming the Philippine's #1 Success Coach. If I can go from broke to becoming a star in my field just by living these principles, anyone can.

Each one of us can have the Midas touch. I've seen it in my clients' lives. Through my motivational courses and coaching programs, I've helped thousands of my countrymen achieve their dreams. Many were living in a hand-to-mouth existence and are now becoming multi-millionaires because of the work that I do.

Sometimes, when my clients who have found success stand next to me on stage and talk to the students in my programs, I'm overcome with emotion. I just have to go to the washroom and cry. As a man, that's a little tough to admit, but it truly touches my heart to help people break through their current limitations and thrive. That feeling is something money can't buy.

My clients and I are living proof that if you work the principles, the principles always work.

THE RICHEST MAN

Forrest Willett

At 31 years old, my life was right on track. I owned three homes and seven businesses, had been married for seven years to a beautiful woman and had a two-year old son. I felt on top of the world. That is, until my world turned upside down. Literally. I was in an automobile accident that threw my car end-over-end three times, leaving me with a catastrophic brain injury.

Suddenly, my beautiful wife was teaching me how to brush my teeth and comb my hair. Although I knew that I was lucky to be alive, I began to spiral faster and faster into a deep pit of depression, anger, and despair.

In the beginning, like a stroke survivor, I had difficulty conversing on even the most basic level. My humiliation rendered me housebound, and soon, fatigue and apathy dominated my existence. For hours, I lay on the sofa, sleeping or watching television. The doctors, my speech therapist, my occupational therapist, my physical therapist—essentially all of the experts—had told me that returning to a productive life with the promise of success wasn't possible, so I gave up all hope of ever having a normal existence— let alone a life that fulfilled my dreams.

What made it worse was my sense of victimhood. I hadn't chosen this overwhelming turn of events; I hadn't even been driving! I'd been the passenger. Talk about being in the wrong place at the wrong time! Every day, I bathed in self-pity: *Poor me. Why did this have to happen to me?* Days turned into months and eventually years. I withdrew from my wife and son, convinced I was of no use whatsoever.

If I had been my wife, I would have left me.

Then one day, as I lay in bed, numbly surfing the TV channels, the words, "If you want to get from where you are, to where you want to be . . . " caught my attention. I sat up enough to focus on what the news anchor was saying. Jack Canfield was "coming up next" to discuss his book, *The Success Principles*. Listening to Jack speak, I knew I did not want to be lying in that bed, burnt out and tired, anymore. With the smallest spark of hope ignited, I bought the book they were talking about—which turned out to be a big, thick book. When I showed it to my speech therapist, she gave me a worried look and said, "Perhaps you're being over-zealous." At the time, I was just learning how to read my son's books—a thirty-five-year-old man reading books for a kindergartener. Yep, I was definitely ready to get from where I was to where I wanted to be. And so, I began my journey.

Even though I was motivated, my progress was slow. I began to wonder if my therapist had been right. Maybe I *was* being overly ambitious . . .

Then, several months after starting to work my way through *The Success Principles*—and a full five years after the accident—I had my biggest wake-up call. It was my son Hunter's seventh birthday party. I was out in the yard with Hunter and a group of his friends, as Hunter opened his presents. Picking a round-shaped one off the pile, he ripped the wrapping paper off to reveal a baseball. Smiling with delight, he immediately threw it at the ground. Naturally, the ball landed with a thud and rolled off a couple of feet in the dirt. Hunter bent down, picked it up, and hurled it at the ground again, where it once more rolled away from him. Before he could try again, the friend who had given him the baseball, shouted, "Hunter, baseballs don't bounce!"

In that moment, the impact my absence had had on my son hit me like a ton of bricks. *How could he know?* We had never tossed a baseball together. I had never taken him to see a baseball game. *Where had I been?* I had spent more time with my negative thoughts than with my son, essentially abandoning him, as well as my wife. I knew that if I didn't take charge of my life, it would end up in pieces. I'd find myself divorced, homeless, or worse.

The spark inside me turned into a blaze. I went back to the first of the Success Principles, *Take 100% Responsibility for Your Life*, and tackled it in earnest. It took me a few months to truly grasp that one. Not only was I filled with self-doubt and negativity about my future, but all the experts agreed with me. "You're as good as you're going to get," they still said. "Accept it. Learn to live with what you have." I *had* lived with that, and for so long that I'd stopped questioning it. Now here was this guy Jack Canfield telling me that if I applied these principles, I could overcome any devastating event. It was as if Jack believed in me! And so I decided to believe Jack more than my doctors—and to do exactly what he said.

In my case, the first step in taking 100% responsibility for my life was stopping the negative self-talk: No more "Poor me" and "Why did this happen to me?" Without that constant negative soundtrack to distract me, I could see that I hadn't been an active participant in my own rehabilitation. I had been letting my physical therapist stretch me, and then wondered why I wasn't getting stronger. I'd sat there passively listening while my speech therapist read to me, and then complained that my reading skills weren't getting any better. *After all*, I'd figured, *the accident wasn't my fault. I shouldn't have to do anything.*

Now I started to believe that my life could be different, that I could make it different. And that's when things really started to change.

Almost immediately, my self-awareness began to grow. Things that had gone over my head for so long finally registered. Where were all my friends? The answer was as painful as it was clear: I'd abandoned them, in the same way I'd abandoned my family. Everyone had stopped calling long ago, pushed away by my negativity, and I'd been too self-absorbed to care. Just noticing these things was a success in itself, I reminded myself. I was making progress.

Next, I decided to give up blaming and complaining—but that wasn't easy: I found it had become so habitual that I didn't even notice when I was doing it. So I asked the people around me to help me become aware when I slipped back into my old habit. My wife and therapists had a sign: if I began to blame or complain, they let me know by pulling on their ear. When I saw that, I'd stop whatever I was saying in mid-sentence, take a deep breath, and consider my next words more carefully.

Not that speaking—positively or negatively—was easy for me. I still hadn't fully regained my speech faculties, and sometimes I was unable to find the words I needed, or I stuttered. Because of this, I didn't want to go to the grocery store, or the post office, in case I ran into someone I knew and they asked how I was doing. To counter this, I focused on Success Principle #22, *Practice Persistence.* Each day I read Jack's book for twenty minutes and practiced stepping out of my comfort zone. Day after day, I practiced a little more and went a little further.

One of my steps out of my comfort zone took me into a local coffee shop. For years I had just put my head down and walked past that coffee shop, keeping my eyes glued to the cement. But this day I walked in—reminding myself of Jack's Principle #15: *Feel the fear and do it anyway.* Unfortunately, I was met right away by my worst fear. An old acquaintance recognized me and called out, "Hey, Forrest, I hear you went a little cuckoo from that accident."

Although I was cringing with embarrassment inside, I stayed calm and just walked over and sat down with him. I explained to him as best I could what had been happening. I was amazed to find it actually felt good to stand up for myself. I tried this with others in the coming days, and with time it got easier. What I discovered was that there were people around me who were willing to support me—especially now that I was willing to support myself.

I also saw that I wasn't alone in dealing with life's fears and challenges. Everyone I talked to seemed to have struggles and pain of their own.

All those years of walking with my head hanging down and studying the ground had let me see that there are cracks in the foundations of buildings everywhere you go. It doesn't matter if it's a multi-million-dollar building or a shack, you can find a crack. Now I saw that it was the same for people; *we* all have cracks in our foundation, too. We all have things we're working on. This insight helped me to overcome the shame I'd been carrying for so long.

In fact, as time passed, I could hardly believe the successes I was having. Within a year of applying Jack's principles, I was doing all of the things the doctors said that I couldn't do. I returned to school. I got off all medications, both for pain and depression. I started volunteering. I started turning every negative into a positive. And I've been doing that ever since.

Today, it's hard to believe there was a time, not that long ago, that I couldn't speak fluently, or read or write very well. I've turned that around so completely I've even been able to write a book about my experiences! I get requests daily to share my story in front of an audience, and I've found I love public speaking. Before the accident, I would never have considered doing any public speaking, and afterward, I wouldn't have dreamed it could ever be possible. Yet today I feel I've found the work I was meant to do; I'm thrilled I get to travel the world to speak to so many wonderful people.

Recently I was able to attend one of Jack Canfield's advanced programs called Train the Trainer (TTT). I had a lot of free-floating anxiety going into it, which was heightened the first day. The level of financial success of the people in the group was very intimidating and I thought, *I'm out of my league here. This isn't for me.* But after hearing everyone share about their lives during the course, I realized something huge: we are all the same. We all have crap in our past that haunts us. We all have problems at home. We all have those cracks in our foundations.

One of the major cracks that came up for me at TTT was in the area of relationships. Before the accident I'd been a happy-go-lucky, fun-loving guy, but I also knew what it felt like to have a broken heart and to be sad and lonely. My mother left home when I was six years old and I had a pretty rough childhood. At fourteen, I moved out of my house to live with an elderly woman down the block and take care of her. When I was sixteen, I moved to another city on my own. I went to school, got a job, paid rent, and started my own successful business. All this created a lot of independence—as well as the belief that the people who are supposed to love you and take care of you, don't.

To protect others from feeling that way, before the accident I'd always made it a point to be there for people and to give love freely and generously. Over the course of my recovery, I'd found my way back to that ability. But at TTT, I realized that I didn't know what it felt like to *receive* love—not even from my own wife. I had been married nearly twenty years by that time, but out of fear of being hurt again, I hadn't learned how to accept her love.

The wall I'd built around my heart became obvious on the very first morning of the course. We were all sitting, notebooks in our laps, pens poised, when Jack announced we'd be starting with what he called "The Silent Hug Process." We were to stand up and mill around the room, giving everyone we met a long, silent, full-body hug, after which we were to look the person in the eyes before moving to the next person.

I felt everything inside me turn to stone. *No way was I going to do this.* I looked toward the door, ready to bolt. Although we had just started, I considered taking an early bathroom break. But by now, Jack's principles had become deeply ingrained. From somewhere inside me I heard, *Forrest, feel the fear and do it anyway.*

I stood frozen as a young man walked up to me and put his arms around me. I let him hug me and even hugged him back, but I could hardly breathe, I was so uncomfortable. After what seemed an hour, but was only about a minute, he stepped back, looked me straight in the eyes and smiled. Staring back at him, I could feel my face burning and my palms sweating, but I forced my lips into a fake smile.

After a few more seconds, he walked away and it took everything I had not to fall over. The next instant, a young woman stood in front of me, and we repeated the process. Hugging her was a little more comfortable, but as I looked into her eyes afterward, I could still feel my heart pounding with fear.

The next person to approach me was a motherly sort of woman. As she gathered me in her arms, I could feel something inside me give. When she stepped back to look me in the eyes, the dam broke and I began to cry. Seeing my tears, she began to cry, too. We hugged again for a long time, and like a child, I let myself relax into the comfort of her loving embrace.

When we finally let go of each other, I smiled at her, a real smile this time, one that came straight from my heart. I could feel the love between us like a warm current.

Taking a deep breath, I turned to the next person. Though tears were still brimming in my eyes, my arms were ready to reach out. The fear was gone, replaced by a pleasure I'd been longing for my whole life.

Each morning, we started with the silent hug process and the joy and happiness I experienced as I hugged person after person filled me to bursting. By the end of the course, I felt transformed and open and connected to others in a way I'd never been before. When I got home, I hugged my wife and son and said, "I've always loved you but I wasn't fully able to let your love in. Now I'm ready." Today, we freely express our love for each other, and I count it as one of my greatest successes.

Reading *The Success Principles* has shifted my thinking about success in general. Before the accident, success for me was all about money: the dollars, the things—a bigger boat and a bigger house, opening more businesses. More money, more stuff. And after the accident I'd given up on ever attaining *any* success, however you define it. But today, thanks to Jack, I've learned the profound truth that having all the stuff in the world doesn't mean anything if you're not truly living—which I now know means giving and receiving love.

For me, that's where the riches are now. If currency were counted in friends and love, I would be the richest man in the world. I was pretty successful before, but since Train the Trainer, I've become a multi-millionaire.

TAPPING INTO TRUST

Dina Proctor

In 2010, I was working as an office manager at a big corporation. It was a comfortable job, with adequate pay, and I even liked it, but I was ready for a change. I'd had a huge internal transformation a few years earlier, in which I'd gone from being a suicidal—though high functioning—alcoholic to being a peaceful, happy, and addiction-free person. My new life was unrecognizable from the one that I had been living and unimaginably joyful.

I wanted to share how I'd made that change with others, in the hopes of inspiring them, but had no idea how that would really work, or even what it would look like. So, like so many good ideas, this one just hung around, like a coat on a hook, waiting for me to put it on. Weeks and months passed, and still no action.

Then one day, as I sat at my desk at work, looking through my inbox, I saw an email from Janet Attwood, an author and teacher who I'd signed up to receive emails from on the basis of an article I'd read by her. The subject line read: Do you want to meet me and Jack Canfield in Maui?

That caught my attention. I didn't really know Janet and I didn't know who Jack was either, though his name sounded familiar. I furrowed my brow, trying to place him. *Hmmm, I think that's the Chicken Soup guy.*

I read on. The retreat in Maui was exclusive—a chance for just a dozen or so people to have time working on their goals and dreams with Jack and Janet. The price was exclusive too: $15K plus travel and accommodations. I didn't have that kind of money—in fact it was almost a third of my salary at the time. But reading that email gave me goose bumps. And try as I might, I couldn't shake the feeling. I wanted to go. A lot.

But I had absolutely no idea how that would or could happen.

Then unexpectedly, I received a call from my financial advisor with huge news: Over half of the money I would need had magically shown up in my life from an investment I'd completely forgotten about!

I immediately registered for Maui. Though I had always been cautious and conservative about spending—saving my money for a rainy day—I knew this was something I needed to do.

The retreat was amazing. The seed of the desire I'd been carrying around for so long sprouted, as Jack and Janet showed me how I could turn my message into a career that could change a lot of people's lives.

Back home from Maui, I began writing a book about my experiences, which was what I had defined as the first step of my new calling during the retreat. The amount of spare time I had to write was miniscule, so making headway on my book was slow. But I was still too chicken to leave my comfortable job to pursue my dream full time. I grew frustrated pretty quickly though and made a promise to myself: within six months, I would make the leap.

A few months later, I received an invitation from Jack's office to attend the taping of a program about the Emotional Freedom Technique (EFT), also called "tapping." Jack had written a book with Pamela Bruner about it, and he and Pamela were looking for a group of people from Southern California to participate in the taping of a DVD about tapping that would be included in their book.

I didn't know what EFT was, but I loved Jack and if he thought it was a good thing, I was game. I agreed to attend.

At the taping, Pamela and Jack asked for volunteers to demonstrate using EFT to work through their limiting emotions or beliefs. I jumped up and went to the front of the room.

To begin, Pamela asked me what breakthrough I wanted to have. This was about six to eight weeks before the date I'd picked to quit working at the corporate office and start spending all my time getting my message out into the world. I said, "I'm scared to death to leave my day job and pursue my real dream."

The fear I had about making this life transition was two-fold: First, I was afraid to share my story with the world because of what people would think of me if I revealed the out-of-control drinking I'd hidden for so many years, and second, I was terrified that I wouldn't be able to pay my bills or survive if I gave up the security of my job.

Pamela showed me the tapping points and then she asked me if the fear I was talking about sat in my body somewhere. I closed my eyes and said, "Actually, yes. It feels like this gigantic lead brick in my stomach. And it extends beyond my physical body."

She asked me a bunch of detailed questions about it. "How heavy is it? What texture is it? Is it sharp or smooth? What color is it?"

I told her, "It's heavy and dark grey and solid with sharp edges."

Next, Pamela and Jack led me through the tapping process, which entails tapping on certain acupuncture meridian points while exploring different ways to reframe the situation psychologically. They explained that it's the combination of simultaneous physical and psychological work that gives tapping its remarkable power.

After just a couple of minutes of tapping, Pamela asked me "Well, how is that dark grey lead brick in your belly now?"

I remember thinking, *Why is she asking me that? I just told her in detail a couple of minutes ago.* But to my surprise, when I checked in on the fear in my stomach, it had changed.

"Do you know what? It feels like a cookie sheet!" I said. "It still has some size to it, but it feels like it's a lot lighter and thinner—like it's movable. Definitely not as heavy or dark."

We continued tapping. After a few rounds of going through the points, Pamela asked me to check in again. "Now it's much lighter," I said, "like a sheet of aluminum foil."

I felt it for a moment and said, "It's weird, but it almost feels like it's being thrown around by waves on the top of a sea."

Jack looked at me and smiled. "Do you know what the sea, or what I'd call the ocean, you're describing represents?" he asked.

I shook my head.

"The ocean describes the power of your Higher Self, the universal power that you're connected to. It's so much bigger than this little problem. It's your perspective that makes the problem seem huge and heavy. In reality, it's just this little thing riding on the ocean of your Higher Self."

And just like that, my fear of quitting my job dissipated. I felt so free! I felt like I could do anything I wanted to do.

In the following days, I was curious to see if the fear would return, as it had been chronic for months and it seemed impossible that it could disappear so quickly. But it didn't come back and still hasn't, to this day. That 10-minute tapping session seems to have dissolved it completely.

A few weeks later, I quit my job. I just trusted and relaxed into faith. Tapping had brought me up to speed for the next chapter of my life. The fear was gone and I was up for it!

I spent the next six months writing my book and then the next six after that getting it edited and ready to launch. On the day it was released, my book, *Madly Chasing Peace: How I Went from Hell to Happy in 9 Minutes a Day*, went to the top of Amazon's bestseller list in its category—yes, all the way to #1! What a thrilling day that was. And what a profound validation of the principles I had been learning. Since then, I've been speaking, coaching, and developing programs for individuals and businesses based on my work.

For me, the tapping session was a breaking-open point, a huge pivotal experience for me. And having once crossed into that new place of trust, I've had access to it ever since. I always know how that feels to be there. When I start to feel any fear, I remember that experience and I know how it will feel to get back into alignment. Then I do the tapping, or whatever inner work is appropriate to get me there.

For months, I had been standing in front of a locked door and I couldn't find the key. I'm so thankful to have had the good fortune to work with Jack and Pamela that day. They handed me the key and I opened that door—and walked straight through into the life of my dreams.

WORTHY OF LOVE

Lisa Nichols

My passion has always been helping people. In 2000, I started my company, *Motivating the Teen Spirit* to empower teens to fall madly in love with themselves. We focus on showing young people how to set healthy boundaries, how to put words to their feelings, and to respond versus react to the things that happen in life. In recent years, I've expanded my mission to include people of all ages, because I believe that all of us deserve to fall in love with the person whose face we see in the mirror each and every morning.

I first learned of Jack Canfield and his work in 2002 when I read a few of the *Chicken Soup for the Soul* books. I loved those books, but I never thought I'd have anything to do with them.

Imagine my shock when, in 2004, I got a call from Jack's long-time friend and student Eve Hogan, who was also one of my good friends. Jack told Eve he really needed a powerful African American person to work on *Chicken Soup for the African American Soul*—someone who was "authentic, transparent, and could take the project by the horns."

Eve said, "I know the person," and she told Jack about me. It turns out Jack had been a long-time admirer of my work with teens.

Eve called me and said, "Jack Canfield wants you to apply to be the co-author of *Chicken Soup for the African American Soul*."

At first, I refused, saying I was too busy. The truth was I was scared. I'd failed writing in high school and wasn't going to put myself in the position to be judged like that again. No way!

Eve called me again and again and each time I said the same thing, "I'm a single mom, I'm a CEO, I'm too busy." Then one day, before I could stop it, the truth slipped out. "And I'm really scared!" But being the coach that she is, Eve walked with me into that fear and convinced me to try again. Even though I was still scared, I wrote up six stories and submitted them to Jack—who loved my work!

That was when I gave my English teacher back her negative opinion about me—which I'd been holding onto for 18 years. I went on to co-author, not just one, but two *Chicken Soup for the Soul* books and my own book, *No Matter What*.

It was through doing the *Chicken Soup* books together that Jack and I became friends. One of the most powerful success principles I've learned from Jack is a terrific feedback exercise that he does with his wife, Inga. He asks her, "On a scale from one to ten, where would you rate our relationship?" Inga rates their relationship: 6, 7, 8, 9—somewhere on a scale of one to ten. No matter what Inga's answer is, the second question he asks is, "How do I make it a 10?"

After hearing about this exercise, I instantly began to use it with my son Jelani, who was 11 years old at the time. I had been really feeling guilty about being separated from him so much due to my work. The first time I asked him to rate our relationship, Jelani gave it a 7. *Hmm*, I thought, *not terrible, but it could sure be better*. Taking a deep breath, I asked, "What would make it a 10?"

He said, "I want to see you more. I want to travel with you."

I took this to heart and committed to find a way to make this happen. First, I enrolled him in a private school, with the condition that Jelani be able to distance-learn while he traveled with me. The school administrators said, "We've never done that before."

I told them, "I'm excited that we get to co-create a new possibility!"

The school agreed to try it and for the next two years Jelani traveled with me whenever he wanted to. I'd show him my travel calendar six months in advance and he'd choose a place that he wanted to go. Eventually he said, "Mom, I'm ready to stay at home." We'd handled that particular part of improving our relationship.

Jelani is seventeen now. I asked him the question just two days ago while we were watching movies together. He said, "Oh, Mom, this again?"

I repeated the question.

He said, "I'd rate it a 9."

I asked him, "What would take it from a 9 to a 10?"

He sat there and he thought and thought and thought. Finally, he said, "I can't think of anything. But it seems so weird to say it's a 10; that would make it perfect."

I said, "Okay, so if it's not perfect, what would make it a 10?"

Jelani said, "All I can think of is sitting on the couch, watching movies with you, our feet touching, and cooking with you. We're doing all that now, but it still feels weird to say it's a 10!"

In that moment, I felt my heart swell up with love. I don't care how many stages I stand on, how many millions of people that I speak in front of, how much wealth I generate—the most important thing to me is the relationship I have with my son. It's beyond price.

Jack gave me a tool to monitor my son's needs, his desires, what he's getting, what he's *not* getting. For that, I'll forever be grateful.

Another place in my life where I'm grateful for Jack's work is in the area of romantic relationships. For a long, long time, I hadn't given attention to my love life: building my business and being a mom had been my priorities. Then one day I looked up, and realized that I was ready. But I wanted to have a *deep and healthy* relationship, not just a relationship. At the time, my mindset was, *I do "girlfriend" really well, but I don't know if I could ever be someone's wife.* I really had this chatter in my mind about being unworthy of long-lasting love.

I struggled with this belief about myself for months, until I attended a workshop at a meeting of the Transformational Leadership Council, a group that Jack founded of teachers, speakers, and thought leaders in the field of personal growth. At the workshop, Jack led us through a very powerful exercise that he uses in his Breakthrough to Success Training. The exercise, called the Tri-Synch Integration Process, is for identifying and releasing limiting beliefs.

To start, Jack had us write down something really big that we believed about ourselves that was standing in our way. I was very uncomfortable. Sharing something so deeply personal made me feel exposed. But everyone was exposing themselves, so I thought, *Oh God, I'll do it, too.* Before I could chicken out, I wrote down the big scary thing that had been rattling around in my head: *I am not worthy of long lasting, forever love.* Okay, there it was in black and white.

Then Jack had us share our limiting belief with the people sitting around us. It wasn't easy to say that sentence out loud, much less to other people, but I did it.

Then he had us write an affirmation, a mantra that could help us reprogram our minds. I wrote, "I am worthy of healthy, long-lasting, *amazing* love." Just writing that affirmation generated lots of emotion for me. I felt goose bumps all over and my heart started beating fast. I was out of my comfort zone, yet I knew that if I could ever truly adopt that belief for myself, it would be huge.

The next step was to break into groups of four to do the tri-synch process together—one person at a time went through the process while the others helped. I was the first person to do it. Jack had my three partners sit around me, one on either side and one behind me. Their job was to say my affirmation out loud to me over and over again, one in each of my ears and the other from the back of my head. The theory is that with your ears busy processing the voices from each side, the voice coming from behind you can slip the affirmation into your subconscious.

I closed my eyes and my group of three began. "*Lisa*, you are worthy of long-lasting, healthy, amazing love. *Lisa*, you are worthy of amazing, long-lasting, healthy love," they repeated. There were two women in my group whose voices were very nurturing. There was also a man named Lee Bauer. (Lee had been in the movie *The Secret* with me.) Lee's strong man's voice bellowed into my right ear. "*Lisa*, you are worthy of long-lasting, healthy, amazing love." The sound of it made my heart beat fast as the tears started streaming down my face, on to my hands. "*Lisa*, you are worthy of long-lasting, healthy, amazing love." My palms got sweaty and I could feel my mind working on it. *Am I? Am I?*

I'd held this limiting belief for years, and had disguised it in *I'm busy being a mom and building this company*. When you're successful enough, people give you a pass for those other things, like having a loving romantic partner. Now, I didn't want that pass anymore. I was giving myself permission, through Jack's instruction, to go for *everything* that was really important to me.

Then the moment came.

It felt like the exercise had been going on three hours, though it had only been a few minutes. *"Lisa,* you are worthy of long-lasting, healthy, amazing love." Suddenly, I felt myself choose to release that limiting belief: *Yes, I am. I am!* I was sobbing so hard. *I am worthy of long-lasting, healthy, amazing love.*

It was the biggest breakthrough. Jack had created a safe space for me to be transparent and it had opened up a set of double doors I literally hadn't been through in over ten years.

Since that day, I've never gone back to the old belief. Instead, I live in the new possibility. I've dated three or four men in the last four years and we've had incredible, breathtaking relationships. Although we're not each other's life-mates, I am still great friends with each of them. We continue to honor and celebrate each other.

Today I know what healthy relationships look like, because of all the work I've done—and especially because of what Jack helped me to see: I am worthy of healthy, long-lasting, amazing love *on all levels*.

NO LONGER FEELING NUMB

Alicja Zajac-Merifield

World War II had broken out in Europe and the soldiers had left a few weeks before to fight on the Front. My mother Margaret was seated in her classroom and was daydreaming, thinking of Mieciu, her only brother and of Leon, her father. Both were gone to fight for their country. That morning, she and her four sisters had comforted their lonely and frightened mother, kissed her goodbye, and had walked the three kilometers to school. Since they were already late, each ran to their classrooms. Little did they know that they would not see each other again until decades later.

There was a disturbance at the classroom door. Alarmed, she looked around. The teacher was distraught, trying to shield the doorway with her body. Two uniformed soldiers roughly pushed her aside and stepped into the classroom. My God. They're the SS, thought Margaret! In clear Polish, one soldier demanded that all the officer's daughters stand up. "Dziewczynki, nie, nie!" (Little girls, no, no!) cried the teacher, as Margaret and a few other girls slowly stood up. The girls were then escorted outdoors and onto a bus. Girls from other classes had already boarded. As Margaret looked towards the back, a little girl saw her and shrieked, "Malgosia!" Margaret's little sister Danusia ran to her and threw her arms around her older sister, sobbing her little heart out. Soon the bus was on its way to Germany where the girls were made to work in fields and factories for the rest of the war. Margaret tried to help her little sister as much as she could. Danusia was fragile and much younger. At night, Margaret would cuddle a sleeping Danusia and thank God that somehow her other three sisters had been spared. Then she would fall asleep exhausted, having done the work of two.

After the war, a Polish officer was combing the rubble in Heilbronn with his men, searching for survivors. In a heap of debris he found a young woman, lying unconscious. When he realized that she was alive, he quickly carried her to the Red Cross camp. Tadeusz visited her daily. They fell in love and were married along with nine other couples. A year later, I was born.

My parents, especially my mother, were very strict with me. As I was growing up, I didn't understand the reason for her severity. Like any teen, I felt resentful and often even believed that she didn't love me. My brother was given much more freedom and I thought that must be because 'boys don't get into trouble the way girls can'. Only much later did I understand that, being a girl, she felt the need to protect me, just as she had tried to protect her little sister from the brutality all around them. But I saw it as being mean and keeping me from things that other girls were allowed to do. I was frequently compared to other girls and told that I was not to be like them. I was told that I was ugly when I was unhappy. When I tried to make cookies and burned them, I was told that I couldn't do anything right. If I didn't get an A or a B, she told me that I was stupid. I wasn't allowed to ride my bike outside of our yard until I was fourteen and even at age seventeen I had to be home from the Prom before midnight. Later, I married the male version of my mother. He kept the bankbook and gave me just enough for groceries. Of course, I cherish my many special and precious memories of wonderful times with mom, but the negative ones are leading towards what I experienced while taking part in a meditation conducted by Jack Canfield.

I was seated in my home taking notes during an online coaching call and Jack stated that he was about to lead a meditation. I sat back in my chair, closed my eyes, relaxed and listened. He took us through a series of steps beginning with breath work, and then began the guided visualization. We were first asked to focus on a place in our lives where we felt stuck or blocked, or a goal we were having trouble reaching, or something we wanted to create in our lives but couldn't do. I immediately felt depleted. My hands hurt and something heavy sat in the pit of my stomach. I thought of the guilt and shame and desperation I had felt ever since I sold my beautiful home in the Oak Hills three years previous. After paying off the large line of credit that had helped me to keep the house for five years, there was no profit left. What an illusion that had been. I now had no savings. I thought of the goal I was determined to reach, that of making three times my salary or better by the end of the year and I wanted to cry.

Jack then asked us to feel where in our bodies we had tension or other discomfort. Then we were to see it and describe it. The tension across both hands and in my solar plexus increased. When I looked inwardly to visualize what was there, I saw heavy rectangular cubes, like black bricks of a hard, viscous substance. We were told to go back in time to when the pain had manifested. What happened next, as I was transported back over sixty years, moved me to the core.

The memory which surfaced was of a small and vulnerable five-year-old Alicja in the summertime, in a small town in northern Ontario. We were new immigrants and I knew no English. The day before must have been a Saturday or Sunday because we had gone out of town to a Fair and I was happily playing outdoors alone with a green, wooden shepherd's crook from which a little stuffed monkey was hanging. I remembered that my dad wasn't home, so he must have been at work.

A boy aged around ten was standing behind a shed and he called to me. I recall being startled and then curious, so I approached him since he seemed to have something that he wanted to show me. He acted as though he wanted to see the little monkey so I let him have the crook. The boy dropped it and grabbed my shoulders, pushed me against the shed and pressed against me. I screamed so he let go of me and ran away. My mother was twenty-four at the time. She came running out of the house and asked what the matter was. I told her that a very bad boy had tried to do something bad. She said I was lying because she didn't see anyone. I started to cry and she made me go into the house. Mom demanded that I tell her the truth so I repeated exactly what had happened, whereupon she started to spank me with the shepherd's crook, telling me that I was a bad girl. To protect my bottom, I put my hands behind me and she hit me across my hands then made me go to bed. I was crying under the covers so she gave me another whack and somehow got me on the hands again, as well as on my stomach.

I remember whimpering because I hurt and because mom didn't believe me even though I had told the truth. Then dad must have come home because I recall that he was in the kitchen with mom then he came out and ran his hand gently across my hair and face, telling me not to cry.

My hands have bothered me for several years and two of the fingers of my right hand in particular have arthritis, right across the knuckles where I had been struck. Frequently, while I am on the computer and especially after I go to bed, my hands feel numb and I have to shake and massage them, then let my arms dangle from the mattress to let the blood flow. Also, over the years I have felt guilty for not being able to hold onto things and letting things slip away . . . my marriage, finances, my dream home, my wonderful, big, amazing goals.

Jack then had us approach the child and talk to her. I approached that little girl and told her that I love her and that I will protect her. I told her that mom was young and did the best she could at the time. I reminded her that mom had been taken from school during the war, placed on a bus with other officers' daughters, and driven to Germany to work in the fields, so she had missed her childhood and was just learning about parenting when she had me, so long ago. I reached out and hugged her and she stopped crying and held on to me. She felt so warm and little . . .

We were then to approach the future 'us', at age eighty-five. I sat with the future me. At eighty-five, I was living my dream, seated at a table in a room with floor to ceiling windows, elegant, confident, smiling gently and dressed beautifully in soft blue and white. I sat across from me and she told me that there was nothing to fear. That incident had happened so long ago and was one of the ingredients of my life. It had made me strong and helped me to understand the pain of others. She pointed to the shelf of books I had now published, and I followed her gaze past the window to the sea beyond. She told me not to give up... to persevere. "This is your legacy", she said, pointing to the books and to paintings on the wall. "Just do it!"

We were brought out of meditation, back to our places. I was immediately aware that my hands were no longer numb. In fact, as I write this, over twenty-four hours have passed and my hands feel wonderful. And the brick in my stomach? It's gone. I felt a ghost of the brick at one point during the day when an issue arose however I was able to smile at the phantom, wish it 'adieu' and it turned into fine mist and disappeared. I believe that it is gone for good.

I am fully confident that, with perseverance, creative thought, determination and hard work, I will achieve the Breakthrough Goal I am working on. I have caught a glimpse of my future and the year 2032 has a wall of books that I have written! I'm excited to discover what my next powerful Breakthrough Goal will be!

By the way, dear mom has Alzheimers and is in a nursing home. She has been there for twelve years. I pray that her thoughts and sensations are gentle, sweet and loving.

I love you, Mama. Ciebie kocham.

FROM LIVING IN THE MISSION TO LIVING MY MISSION!

Logan Doughty

In July 2010, I was sitting outside a homeless shelter, awaiting intake into a long-term, no-frills recovery program. I had recently fallen flat on my face due to alcohol and drugs. Not so long before, I had been a machinist with a wife and child and an above-average income.

When my daughter had been born, I'd been sure I'd be able to control my alcohol consumption. But even with such a strong motivation, I was unable to quit drinking and I was forced to move out of my home. My parents and siblings wouldn't take me in, and I couldn't control my drinking or my temper long enough to have anyone do any more than show me the door.

When I realized that no matter what it cost me, no matter how bad things got, I wasn't going to be able to stop drinking, I went into a deep depression. I knew that I could take my life if I needed to—I actually had a solid plan to do so—yet I put it off. I assumed my daughter might like to have me around if I could straighten myself out. So I decided to try the recovery program at the local rescue mission.

That's when I found myself sitting with the group of men at the door of the shelter, waiting to get inside. I was emotionally spent, physically tired, and seriously stressed. The smell of alcohol was all around me, as well as a constant stream of profanity. Some of the guys were silent and withdrawn; others clustered together, talking quietly—intelligent guys with nowhere else to go—but many were stoned or drunk: obnoxious, angry, swearing, and stinking. This was not going to be easy.

I'd never been in a shelter before, but I soon discovered that everyone is exhausted. The transients are not allowed to be at the rescue mission during the day. They can only sleep there at night. The shelter gives them breakfast and then they're out the door at 7 am. From that time until the late afternoon when they can come back, they're out walking around all day, trying to find a place to sit down. Sometimes they go to the library or hang out in a park. If it's cold, they're cold. If it's hot, they're hot. Life is stripped down: Get up. Get food in your belly. Get going and do what you gotta do to get through this day.

As a participant in the recovery program, I didn't have to leave each morning. The "program" men worked at the Mission all day to pay for our privileges (a room with four roommates, a dresser, and meals). At first, my assignment was to clean the bathrooms, halls, and floors all day. Though some of my tasks were disgusting and repulsive, the work was actually stabilizing.

What threw me into despair was receiving the occasional note from my wife about my daughter's milestones—her first words, first steps. Being disconnected from everything I valued and knowing that I could *never* get those times back was excruciating. I didn't know if I could make it.

Yet, as the months went by at the Rescue Mission, my head cleared little by little, and with the help of a 12-step program and some kind, but strict, Christian, souls, I began to see that I *might* be able to recover from this devastating chapter in my life.

Even one of the worst things about living at the shelter—being surrounded by destitution and death at every turn—provided a strange sort of motivation for me. The fact is, people die at the mission all the time. Whenever it happens, the staff put a Xerox of the deceased's intake picture on a board, have a moment of silence, and then everyone gets on with their business. Most often there's no service, no place to pay respects, no one to contact or to send a condolence letter to. Billy, Larry, John, Willie—men I came to know—passed away with no fanfare. One day they were there, and then they were gone. It was as if they slipped underwater without a splash and disappeared.

Like everyone else, I just accepted it at the time. That's the way things were. But something in me became determined not to die in that way. Especially for my daughter's sake. Given her genetic disposition for alcoholism, I didn't want my sad story to provide her with an easy excuse for drinking.

Though I was far from serene at the Mission, I found that I could bear the daily routine. My family started to have me over occasionally, and actually seemed to want me around. At Christmas that year, my sister gave me a copy of Jack Canfield's book *The Success Principles*. I thought it was sort of corny, but I thanked her nonetheless and added it to my stack of books to read.

At the Mission, there's more TV than a person can stand. It's a great pacifier, I guess, but I didn't watch it. Instead, I read—a lot. Finally, I came to the thick book with the white-haired guy on the front that my sister had given me. I respect my sister, so I knew this wouldn't be garbage, but I was far from sold. I thought, *You can tell the guy's rich. You just have to look at his haircut. How can he know what I'm going through?* And, sure enough, it starts off with a description of the riches and accomplishments of the guy on the cover. I didn't make it through two pages. I told myself, *This book doesn't apply to me. It's for successful people who want to make billions, instead of millions.* So I put the book down.

But eventually I gave it another try. This time, I started by reading the Table of Contents, then skipped the introduction which had stopped me last time and went directly to the Success Principles themselves. To my surprise, Jack seemed like a real guy. He wasn't born rich, and he satisfied my cynical side by explaining in painstaking detail the process by which normal people could actually change their lives. Plus, there were lots of examples.

I continued reading Jack's book every day and even doing the exercises he suggests. Then, on March 26, 2011, at 9:11 p.m., I had an 'AHA!' moment that will stay with me forever. I was sitting at the monitor's desk reading the chapter in *The Success Principles* about deciding what you want in your life. In it, Jack recommends making a list of 20 things you love to do. It sounded simple enough, but working on that list was a completely new experience for me.

In the past, I'd tried to come up with ideas for making money; it had never occurred to me to think about what *I enjoyed* and *what I wanted* to do.

I grabbed a piece of paper and started writing my list: 1) *Exercise,* 2) *Kung-fu,* 3) *Ride my bike,* 4) *Teach self-defense.* When I jotted down 10) *Encourage people,* suddenly, it all clicked into place. I knew what I wanted to do: Create and Teach a Self-Defense System for Women! Everything that had happened to me made sense and I saw I was uniquely suited to help others in a very specific way.

For years I'd been a serious martial artist; I'd already started developing a self-defense program for women, but with my descent into alcoholism, the discipline and honor which is so vital to the martial artist had drained away along with my self-respect.

During Jack's exercise, I'd discovered my purpose or at least an obvious connection between my past and a potential future. I saw that my past fighting experience combined with my newfound energy and focus would make it possible for me to teach my class for a living.

Until that moment, though I'd known that I was basically a good person and that this potential was in me, I hadn't been able to utilize it or tap into it. I couldn't make sense of the violence and anger and hardship I'd experienced. How had this happened to me?

Now I saw that while it was painful, it had made me exceptionally qualified to stand up in front of a group of women and speak to them with authority and understanding. I had witnessed what happened to women on the street and in shelters, seen the strong prey on the weak. Without that experience, I'd just be an academic—someone who'd studied the martial arts, but had never applied them in real life situations, under duress and trauma. Understanding this created a spiritual awakening in me.

It was like being struck by a thunderbolt.

Since that moment, I have looked at people differently. I've treated people differently—with so much more compassion, tolerance, and patience. I want to help people that the old me would have wanted to punch in the nose . . . literally. Before, I was comfortable meeting aggression with aggression. You messed with me and you regretted it. Now, I find I can walk away. I can joke about it. When I stopped feeling sorry for myself, I no longer assumed everyone was out to get me.

Today, I am happily looking for how the world will do me good, rather than supporting my destitute state with negative validation at every turn. I am no longer a victim! This transition is the most powerful thing that has happened in my adult life and I still get excited when I think about that moment.

In September of 2011, I left the Rescue Mission—armed with nothing but a bicycle, clothes, and the newfound knowledge that I can change my environment—inner and outer. I started a small yard-cleaning business that took right off and I'm also a kitchen manager at a restaurant, all of which is keeping me very busy.

Not long ago, the Mission paid for me to attend a nationally recognized instructor certification program for MOAB™ (Management Of Aggressive Behavior.) Since then I have been donating a portion of my time working in an instructor position at the facility. I do this to give back to the establishment that helped save my life. As their official Self-Defense Instructor, I teach volunteers and staff—both men and women—how to deal with disruptive and potentially dangerous behavior at the facility. Slowly but surely, I am moving in the direction of fully developing and teaching my self-defense program full-time.

I owe so much of this success to having read *The Success Principles* right when I needed to hear what it said. That and the 12-step program have transformed me. Now, I understand I can strengthen my family relationships and be there for my daughter. I'm free to move and grow in any direction I choose and set my mind to.

I know who I am. I know where I'm going. And that can never be taken away.

JUST SAY NO!

Mickey Sims

Not long ago, I found an old picture of myself, taken in 1961 when I was seven years old. It's Christmas Day, so I'm wearing my best clothes—a new sweater and what looks like a Panama hat, though probably a fishing hat, cocked at a rakish angle. My socks are pulled up over the cuffs of my pants. Must have been my idea of a styling dude! Makes me laugh to look at it now, but I see something else in that picture that makes me respect that quirky kid: I'm wearing brand new boxing gloves, and I'm standing proudly next to my Huckleberry Hound punching bag. You see, even at that young age, I knew exactly what was important to me. Over the years, I lost sight of that. But thanks to Jack Canfield's book, *The Success Principles*, I've worked my way back to what I knew when I was seven.

By the time that picture was taken, in our living room where I grew up in British Columbia, I'd been boxing for three years. My dad starting teaching me when I was just four years old. He was a boxer, so I guess boxing is in our blood. Still, I set my boxing gloves aside to play hockey through high school, and didn't pick them up again until after I started my career with the British Columbia Sheriff Service as an adult.

For a few years, I trained at a boxing club in the town where I lived. Then when my coach was injured and couldn't continue his position, I was asked to take over. I coached great kids over the years, some of them going on to the Canadian National Championships. I was so proud of those young boxers, many of them at-risk youth. But at the same time, there was definitely a part of me that felt I'd given up on my own dream.

Perhaps to compensate, I threw myself into my day job, working my way up through the ranks of Deputy Sheriff, Sergeant, Staff Sergeant, and Inspector. As part of my work I developed and taught Personal Safety and Awareness programs for bank employees, a Violence in the Workplace workshop for court registry staff, and Safety Tactics for park rangers. It was a great career.

After I retired, I stayed active at the boxing club. It was there that a friend in one of my fitness and boxing classes introduced me to *The Success Principles*. Her expertise was in Team Building and Leadership, a topic that fascinated me. So after she started sharing some of Jack's ideas with me, I worked through his book, digesting different parts of it to help me identify both my life goals and my boxing goals. Though I already knew a lot of the principles in the book, something about the way Jack describes these ideas helped organize them more powerfully in my mind.

There was one chapter that I read over and over again: "Principle 4, Believe It's Possible." In it, Jack writes about a man who won a national kickboxing title after only six weeks of training in that sport. From the very first time I read that chapter, I knew that I wanted to win a national boxing title. That was the start of my adventure! Other chapters helped me navigate my way to fulfilling that goal. One of the most significant was "Principle 42, Just Say No!"

For a long time, my life had centered on my family, my work, and going to the gym. I just wanted to get from day to day without too many problems. The gym was key to that. It was a safe haven for me, a place where I could escape any outside pressure. But now I knew that I could do more with my training than merely escape.

I'd always made time for everyone else. Now I had to say *no* even to coaching boxing, something I loved. But it was time to say *yes* to my own dream. When I started saying *no*, I saw that it's both one of the hardest and easiest things to do. How do you say *no* to a friend who just wants to get together to talk over coffee or a beer? But that's what I did, at least for a while, and suddenly I had all kinds of time for my own training.

Once I made the commitment to achieve my boxing goals and found that time for the required training, "Principle 24, Exceed

Expectations" taught me one more significant lesson. I know I'd heard about the importance of going the extra mile. But reading it here, everything clicked. I found out how long other boxers trained in each of their sessions every day, and I trained fifteen minutes longer than any of them.

Part of my training plan was to lose enough weight so I could box in the middleweight category. This wasn't easy, because I'd been weight lifting, so a lot of my weight was in the form of muscle—a lot harder to get rid of than burning off fat. I had to give up all alcohol. I didn't drink even an ounce, and I cut way back on food. In just three months, I lost the required thirty-eight pounds. Plus, every day I visualized myself winning a major boxing title, and used that goal in my affirmations.

Bottom line: the success principles worked! In 2011 I won the Ringside World Senior Masters Middleweight Boxing title in Kansas City, Missouri, and the next year I defended my title. Now I've set my sites on the Highland Games. Jack's book let me see that I could have everything I wanted once I learned to say *no*. That one act was the foundation that cleared the decks and gave me the space to go for my dreams again. When I look back at that kid next to the Huckleberry Hound punching bag, I can see now that he wasn't going to be satisfied with anything less.

INVESTING IN MYSELF

Pamela Bruner

"Listen to this." I nudged my husband Dave with my foot, interrupting him yet again. "You've got to let me read you this part."

Dave raised his eyebrows, set aside his own reading material, and gave me his undivided attention again.

That's the way we had spent the entire Saturday afternoon, sitting in the living room as I shared fascinating tidbits and enlightening stories from the new book I'd picked up, *The Success Principles*. In an effort to start a new business, I'd read a lot of books, but this new one by Jack Canfield, America's #1 Success Coach, was the most helpful. It was a masterful collection of reframes, ideas, and guidelines. I loved the way it was organized in small chunks and found myself going back over it again and again for guidance and inspiration.

I needed both.

Although my career as a professional Celtic harpist was successful by any musician's standards, my schedule was grueling and I did more traveling than I wanted, performing as well as selling the twenty albums I'd made. The music industry was changing and I was reluctant to follow. Instead, I found a field that resonated with me more than music did: coaching. I was already teaching motivational workshops in the music community and moving into coaching seemed natural.

Honestly, though, for four years I stumbled around with what I now call "an imaginary coaching business." Selling albums was comfortable and contributed to my income, but fear prevented me from fully marketing my coaching services. I recognized my efforts were half-hearted; I had too many misgivings and beliefs that were out of alignment with growing a business.

In December of 2008, I finally invested in myself by attending a marketing event and hiring an expensive coach—investing nearly five times what I'd ever made by coaching—to help me stay in the business. I laid it all on the line; I was no longer willing to dally around; failure was no longer an option. The $25,000 I'd committed to growing my career yielded $50,000 by the end of the first year. Putting everything on the line, committing without security, really upped my game.

But one of the major game changers came that summer, August of 2009, when I attended Jack's live training, Breakthrough to Success. That's where I really learned to spread my wings and fly. It was a bit of a stretch financially because, by now, I had my husband's full attention and he, too, was going. Together, we had studied and practiced Jack Canfield's principles, which often cropped up in our conversations.

"'Ask! Ask! Ask!'" I would quote.

"'Don't complain unless you're talking to somebody who can do something about it,'" Dave might say.

"'Find a wing to climb under,'" we told each other.

The two of us even had instituted an evening review to acknowledge ourselves every single night. At the end of each day, we sat facing each other.

"It was a good day," I started. Dave simply smiled and listened as I acknowledged the things I was grateful for, listing them one by one, always remembering to recognize at least one of my personal achievements. Then he took his turn, doing the same. This one exercise made a huge difference in our happiness levels—we were putting our attention on what was working in our lives instead of our problems—and in our relationship.

The things we read in Success Principles began to inform and shape my business practices. As someone who needed and sought security my entire life, I began to recognize it doesn't really exist; only the illusion of security exists. Instead, I got excited about success, the idea of dreaming big. "'Take 100% responsibility for your life,'" I reminded myself—realizing with a jolt that I was living and breathing Jack's principles in my daily life, rather than just thinking about them as ideals.

Dave and I were eager to take Jack's teaching to the next level, and the live training seemed the perfect way to do that.

A few months after BTS, I was ready for my first big launch, hoping for fifty people in my coaching program. Yet, after a great deal of work and preparation, with the start date less than a week off, I had only sixteen registered. The outcome looked grim.

Are you going to give up? I asked myself. *Or are you going to fight tooth and claw to get what you can before your deadline? You've got six days. Who knows what you can pull off.*

When a friend urged me to put together an online video, I plunged into the technological research. Within twenty-four hours, I created several videos in a last-ditch publicity campaign. It worked! More than ninety people registered for my program, a huge win!

I didn't give up, I didn't stop, and I kept on not stopping. I fought through my insecurities.

Dedicated to personal growth, Dave and I went on to attend the Advanced Breakthrough to Success, and then Jack's Platinum Mastermind Group. The continued support and help we received there kept us in the conversation. I reframed and transformed both my self and my business.

Practice persistence. Ask! Ask! Ask! Look at what you can do next. Be willing to pay the price. Experience fear and take action anyway. These *Success Principle* messages became daily mantras as I incorporated them into everything I did.

Through my coaching business, I continue to meet a lot of people who dream about playing a bigger game. About having an amazing life. About being a celebrity or making a difference in a huge way. Like me, they need to face what isn't working, learn what's holding them back, and be willing to overcome their obstacles to make the necessary changes. And that's the work I focus on in coaching: teaching others to confront their fears—the gamut of doubts, qualms, and misgivings that have the power to rein us in and prevent us from doing all we can do, creating all we can create. Being all we can be.

TAKING IT TO THE NEXT LEVEL

Mejo Okon

Sometimes, when you're doing something new, you just need a little help to get going. It's like your mom or dad holding the handle bars when you're learning to ride a bike. You can do it, but that support gets you started, builds your confidence, and then off you go.

That's how it was for me and painting. Although I had what it took, I needed a little extra support to set me squarely on the road to success.

I came to being a painter later in life. I was a kid who could draw well from day one, but my parents were depression babies, and for them it was important that I have a job with a specific income. They were adamant that I use my talent for something practical. They didn't want me to end up a starving artist.

When I went to college I found that design was easy for me, so that became my focus. This led to a degree in graphic design and a successful, if varied, career that included advertising illustration, graphic design, being a costume manager for traveling Broadway shows, and even a stint as a courtroom sketch artist. I liked what I did, but there was always that little inner voice that said, "Paint." So I dabbled in it here and there, making birthday cards or gifts for special people, but still mostly drawings.

The years passed, and before I knew it, it was time for my husband John to retire. At that point, we were living in the Midwest, and I was a principal in an internet company. But when John said, let's go, let's do something else, I saw my chance to finally paint. So I retired along with him.

We decided to move to San Angelo, Texas, a small town right in the middle of ranching country. This was the fulfillment of another lifelong passion. I grew up when westerns were popular on television, and I'd always loved the whole idea of cowboys, horses, and cattle. I still have my boots from when I was three years old, and my old cap guns. As an artist, I was drawn to the wide open landscapes, the quality of light and the colors unique to the American Southwest.

Once we were settled, I rented a studio space, and began painting, mostly watercolor and acrylics. I had never really done any oil painting, but a guy in town was giving a class, and he invited me to sit in. After observing the class for a couple hours, I thought, *I can do this*. And that was it: my dabbling days were over and I started painting seriously.

I joined the San Angelo art club where there were monthly exhibitions, classes and seminars to learn different techniques, and ample opportunities to compare notes with other artists. Meeting and talking to people there who'd been painting for a long time, I realized that I had a natural gift. What seemed so difficult for others came easily to me. Soon, I began winning the art club competitions.

Over the next couple of years, my routine progressed. I moved to a studio in an art center where I got more exposure. Then I entered a national contest sponsored by one of the large art magazines that specializes in the southwest genre of painting. They picked ten winners, including me, and published our work. Naturally I was thrilled and excited. This was confirmation that I was on the right path.

Then I hit a plateau. I knew I had talent, but that wasn't enough. I wanted to make a name for myself in the art world. I wanted to make a living with my painting, but I was stalled. Something was missing.

One day I saw a pop-up ad online—probably on Facebook—that said something like "Do you want to take your life to the next level?" It was for a coaching program with Jack Canfield. I'd heard of Jack, but I didn't know he had a coaching program. I kept scrolling, but that ad got me thinking. Although I'd never heard of an artist taking a self-help class or reading a self-help book, maybe this was just what I needed.

I read Jack's book, *The Success Principles*, to make sure his approach would be a good fit for me, and thought his step-by-step instructions for success were great. And the coaching program sounded exactly like what I wanted to do. I'm the kind of practical person that people turn to for advice, so I've often found myself in the role of coach with friends. I've always said that I needed a "me for me," because it's really hard to coach yourself—especially the follow-through. I really wanted somebody to be accountable to.

I was surprised to find out that you don't just enroll for Jack's coaching. They have to be sure you're a good candidate for this kind of program. So I sent in my application and waited.

Right around then, John and I decided to move again, this time to Fort Worth. We were ready for something new and Fort Worth seemed perfect: it's a fun cowboy town with an active and growing art community, and I thought my paintings would fit right in. We started looking for a place to live there and found one we liked immediately. Offers were made and accepted—everything just clicked!

By the time I got the call that I was accepted into Jack's coaching program, we were already in the process of moving. I told Wade, the man who had been assigned to be my coach, that with the move, I didn't know if I could enroll right then.

He said. "Sure, you can!"

I liked his style right away. Wasn't that just what I needed? Someone to say, "You can do it!"? So I said okay, and we began the coaching.

In our first interview, I told Wade briefly about some of my goals for painting. He listened and then asked, "Are you any good?" I hesitated, then said I didn't know. Winning awards in the San Angelo art club was important to me, but taking it outside the club, to a national level, that was a different story. I wasn't totally sure I could compete in that arena.

Coaching started with making a bucket list of all I wanted to do. From that list, I picked one big gigantic goal—recognition on a national scale—and a couple of smaller goals—to be shown in a gallery in Santa Fe, and get accepted in a couple of specific juried art shows. Wade helped me harness the energy needed to accomplish those goals by breaking them down into smaller action steps and then holding me accountable. He was the one who said, what are you doing, and by when? Give me a time. Once a week I'd get to tell him what I'd done, and I loved that. Being an artist is a solitary profession, but reporting to Wade made it like performing for an audience.

With his coaching I was able to prepare paintings and apply for shows that I'd never applied to before. And I got a portfolio ready by doing one painting a month specifically for each show.

Another major part of the coaching process was learning to organize my days. When we moved to Fort Worth, we found a place in an up-and-coming arts area. My studio was in one end of the living space, which worried me a little. I have a great husband who likes to cook for me, and to go out and do things together. That's one of the things I love about him, but I was afraid in this open studio set up that it would be a major distraction. With coaching I learned to set boundaries on my time, scheduling specific days for paperwork or running around and days that are reserved solely for painting. That helped me, and it especially helped my husband. He knew that on certain days, "don't even ask her."

With Wade's help, I also learned to use my time better—turning off my phone when I wanted to focus on my work, limiting my internet use till after 6 p.m., and saying no to the requests that would take me away from my bigger goals.

I started to see results right off the bat. Southwest Art magazine, a national leader in western art, contacted me about being one of twelve artists in a feature article on "Women Artists of the West." And my work was shown at one of only twelve booths at the annual National Cowgirl Museum Induction Ceremony, a chance to debut my paintings in front of the movers and shakers of Fort Worth.

But after only nine months in our new home, a developer bought the building where we lived and decided to demolish it, so my husband and I moved again, this time to Albuquerque, where I have family.

One of the big things I got from Jack's work was his principle, "Ask, Ask, Ask," if you want something, ask for it. If you get a no, you're no worse off than if you hadn't asked! Right after moving to Albuquerque, I put this simple, but sometimes scary, principle to the test.

I drove the hour north to Santa Fe, and walked into a gallery on Canyon Road, the famous Santa Fe street where all the finest southwestern art is sold. I asked to see the owner, *asked* if I could show her a sample of my work and then asked if she would represent me. The answer was YES! And I'm selling work—I've sold a dozen paintings through that gallery in the last six months. The gallery also took my work to a big international art market in Los Angeles, a juried event, and they're putting my work in other shows coming up. That's tremendous exposure for me, on a national level.

Today, as I look around my studio and see the walls covered with paintings of cowboys and their horses, prize cattle, agave cactus, and ranches perched on cliffs, I marvel at how far I've come.

I'm excited for the future as I pursue new and bigger dreams. And though I'm finished with the coaching program, I know the tools I learned there—the organization, scheduling, and goal-setting—will be instrumental in helping me achieve whatever I set out to do.

Elite athletes have coaches, so should artists!

MY STORY OF REINVENTION

Tresa Leftenant

I was driving through an afternoon thunderstorm. The tears flowing down my cheeks matched the raindrops sliding down the window. It was the summer of 1998 and I had just been turned down for a much needed promotion at work. My mounting credit card debt, problems with my deadbeat boyfriend, and my children acting out were overwhelming me with feelings of hopelessness and fear. I pulled over to the side of the road and looked up at the sky through my tears, "Help me out here, God. I don't know what to do. What is it about me that has me experiencing the same problems over and over again in my life?

I moved to Boise, Idaho, in the summer of 1996 after accepting a job as a financial advisor for a regional bank. I left Colorado Springs with hope for a new life after a painful divorce. Moving was my way of escaping the feelings of guilt and shame from my third failed marriage. I had all the same hopes and dreams that every bride has as I walked down the aisle with the man of my dreams four years earlier. Unfortunately, dreams can be smashed in a moment. One morning, I received the call that every person dreads. My husband was at the hospital. He had a car accident as he drove home from an outing with his hiking club. He and two female acquaintances were hit head-on by a family vacationing from India, the father mistakenly driving on the wrong side of the road. The women my husband was driving with were killed and the resulting court case, along with a serious head injury, caused increasing emotional mood swings for my husband. They say that crisis can either bring you closer or pull you apart. At this time in our lives, the latter became our reality.

My life in Boise seemed to go well for a while, on the outside. I was promoted to regional sales manager and the increase in salary allowed me to buy a house of my own. My new job required me to travel around the country, supervising financial advisors and collaborating with other management teams. I felt in over my head much of the time, with the demands of balancing my job and the responsibility of being a single mom with two small children. I coped with feelings of inadequacy and overwhelm by drinking, shopping, and avoiding the truth about my life. I justified my mounting credit card debt with the belief that I had to have the best furnishings in my house and a closet full of high-fashion work clothes to prove and sustain my authority at work . . . and at home.

During those years, in the nineties and living in Boise, I was on a treadmill of spending more to keep up the façade, and needing more income to pay my mounting credit card bills. I kept reaching for the next promotion, and subsequent higher income, to solve my problems. I worked more hours and spent less and less time with my children. I justified my behavior by convincing myself that I was a great role model for hard work and financial achievement. I was in denial on all fronts in my life. My boyfriend was a poor replacement for my children's biological fathers and the growing strife between them when I was at work contributed to my children developing low self-esteem. I walked on eggshells, patching up their quarrels in the evening, convincing myself that the Band-Aid of buying them a new toy or an ice cream was a permanent fix. I just didn't know how to face the unsustainable life path that I was on. It was much easier to ignore my problems.

But that day driving through the rain, when I didn't get that promotion, I did what most people do when they have nowhere else to turn. I cried out for help—without realizing that I'd been receiving help all along.

It's easy to see the yellow alerts I had been getting now, but I was blind to them at the time. My daughter entered junior high in 1998 and began to hang around with the wrong crowd. My son was struggling in grade school, diagnosed with a learning disability. I was in a constant battle with my boyfriend over his unwillingness to work, which led to his bouts of heavy drinking and abusive behavior. I remember having thoughts like, "I have such bad luck," "Why do I always end up with men who won't work?" "Why don't my children just do what I tell them?" "Why doesn't my boss realize my true contribution and give me a raise?" These thoughts only confirmed my victim mentality and excused me from taking any responsibility for my life.

As I was looking up at the sky with tears flowing and the rain pouring, I asked the Universe to help me understand why I kept experiencing the same problems over and over in my life. My problems were always solved with my making more money. In my mind, I had already paid down the credit card debt and taken my family on a lavish vacation. So there I was on the side of the road, feeling a deeper level of shame, guilt, and hopelessness than I had ever felt before. The house had been dropped on my head. The question was whether it would get my attention. Luckily, as I sat in the car crying and thinking, I began to receive the beginning of a new awareness.

I was at the bottom. My usual methods of avoiding the truth had failed and I couldn't see my way out of all of the mess in my life. A new thought began to dawn on me. Since I was the common denominator in all my messes, perhaps it was me that would have to change if I was to have a different life. As I began to feel the truth of that new thought, I said to the Universe, "Ok, I get it. Just show me what to do. I'll do anything to change my life and help my children."

I was very clear as I spoke to the Universe that day. I was ready to stop doing whatever it was that was making my life a mess. I vowed to pay attention, take whatever guidance was given to me, and do my best to integrate it. You might think that this kind of letting go would produce more fear than I already had. Actually, the opposite happened. I felt calm, with a new sense of optimism about the future as I steered my car back onto the road and headed for home.

Less than a week later, I received a brochure, mailed to me by my sister, about a class to help teens learn how to raise their self-esteem. I didn't know much about self-esteem at the time, so I decided to do some research, ready to keep my promise to do anything to help my daughter change the direction of her life.

Around the same time, my boss sent me to a workshop on communication skills. At the break, I picked up a book on tape called *How to Build High Self-Esteem* by Jack Canfield. I thought to myself, *This is curious*, seeing a book about self-esteem when I was considering a course on the same topic for my daughter. I decided to buy the book in order to understand more. I remember opening the set and pushing the cassette in the car tape player on the way home from the workshop.

I was completely transfixed by the introductory story about a group of modern Buddhists in Thailand who discovered a 10 foot tall solid gold Buddha that had been hidden by a layer of clay for more than 300 years. Jack said that just like that statue, we all have a golden essence hidden inside us, and that self-esteem comes from a love that we develop for the unique talents and gifts that we are born with. He went on to say that a lack of self-esteem is the root of many of our problems, including crime, drug abuse, and living lives that don't reach our potential. This was the first time I ever considered that I might have valuable gifts inside me—gifts that were unique only to me and that were put there by Spirit to be shared with the rest of the world. Could it be possible that I had low self-esteem too? Could that be the root of my problems with money, men, and parenting?

Over the next few weeks, I listened to my self-esteem tapes, secretly, over and over in my car. With each story of transformation, I felt more hopeful, and Jack's words seemed to be speaking only to me. I enrolled my daughter in the weekend self-esteem class, called "Walkin' the Talk" and taught by Sue Wade, a school friend of my sister. Sue is a gifted woman devoted to helping troubled teens change the direction of their lives. The content of her weekend workshop for teens centered on helping them identify their unique inner gifts and learning valuable success skills for life. The workshop was experiential. Sue and her team used action-style exercises designed to help kids learn from their experience of themselves.

During the last day of the workshops, parents were invited to attend and to do a few exercises with our children. As my daughter and I sat knee to knee, looking into each other's eyes, we were guided to speak our fears and hopes for each other out loud. By speaking honestly and courageously to each other, for the first time in a long time, we began to build a new foundation of trust that would serve us well as she transitioned from her teens to adulthood. Gina connected to her inner gifts that weekend and increased her self-esteem. Subsequently, she felt a desire to help other kids who were headed in the wrong direction. She went on to participate in many "Walkin' the Talk" teen weekends as a staff assistant. I believe this workshop was pivotal in giving her the confidence and drive to achieve her dream of becoming a doctor. As I write this in July of 2013, Gina just completed her residency and is a board certified internal medicine doctor. She is starting her first job as an associate professor of medicine at a prestigious medical residency program.

The change in my relationship with Gina after the workshop was so dramatic that I tearfully thanked Sue, the facilitator, on the phone several weeks later. I shared with her that I was listening to Jack Canfield's self-esteem book on tape and that it was having a positive impact on my life as well. I was surprised to learn that her teen workshop was based on studies of Jack's work and years of attendance at a weeklong workshop he facilitated every summer in Santa Barbara. I wondered if it was a coincidence that I discovered Jack's book at a seminar and soon met a woman who had learned from him (in Boise, Idaho!), or was it the beginning of a series of synchronistic events sent by the Universe at my request?

Not long after my conversation with Sue Wade, my company sent me to a conference in Chicago. There were several main stage speakers and a few breakout sessions that we could attend by choice. As I was reading the bios of the speakers and deciding which sessions to attend, I noticed that one of the speakers mentioned his training with Jack Canfield. I felt a moment of recognition and a strong inclination to attend his lecture. After his talk, I asked the speaker about his experiences learning from Jack. Just like Sue, he described the weeklong training in Santa Barbara as having a profound and positive impact on his life. I decided right then that no matter what it would take, I would be attending that workshop!

I attended Jack Canfield's Self-Esteem Facilitating Skills seminar in 1998. I participated in over one hundred exercises designed to increase my self-esteem, and learned how to facilitate those same self-esteem building techniques with other groups. Newly empowered, I now had the courage to ask my boyfriend to move out, as well as help my son with additional learning support. I had asked the Universe for answers and guidance to a better life. It was clear to me then, as it continues to be now, that all we need to do to have our dreams come true, is to be clear about our desire to learn and to pay attention to the opportunities that arrive in our day.

Over the last fifteen years, I've become empowered by attending classes and workshops with many life masters in the area of personal growth and spiritual development. The day I asked for help from the Universe, my life began to change. My willingness to be open to life lessons that I needed to learn, led to a healthier relationship with money, my children, my career, and a better life. As my esteem for my unique gifts grew, I no longer needed to keep up the façade of fake wealth and success. I learned to accept the real circumstances of my life, and to learn and implement proven strategies to achieve real financial success. Paying off tens of thousands of dollars in shameful credit card debt gave me new personal power that led me to open my own business, build a seven-figure net worth (and counting), and design programs to empower others to begin their journey to an authentic and prosperous life.

My story wouldn't be complete if I didn't mention the reinvention I enjoy in the rest of my life. As I healed my low self-esteem and learned how to be authentic, honest, and live with integrity, I attracted a relationship with a man who has similar qualities and values. My current husband and I met as graduates of Spectrum, a personal development training modeled after the Lifespring trainings conducted in California and around the world. In January, we celebrated the beginning of what is truly a blessed relationship that began fourteen years ago. He bought a date with me at a bachelor/ bachelorette auction, which we were both guided to attend by what could only be called significant divine guidance. Blessings can show up in ways that we never believe could be possible. It's only when we are open to the possibilities of life that we are guided to these blessings.

My life is beautiful, fulfilling, and blessed in every way. Remembering all we have shared together as a family brings me to my knees in a prayer of gratitude. When I think back to my frame of mind in that car back in Boise, and how fortunate I am to have made such a massive transformation in my life, more gratitude prayers flow. I now serve on Jack Canfield's assisting team and bring as many family and friends as I can to his workshops and trainings. I have the honor and privilege to give back to the first mentor that arrived in my life, and to support others on their quest for happiness, success, and joy. Hopefully my story will inspire you to a similar personal journey of self-discovery and reinvention, one that will lead you to the attainment of a much-deserved life of your dreams.

DON'T GIVE UP

Heather O'Brien Walker

I was ecstatic about figuring out all the details for my upcoming wedding and at the same time I was jumping in with both feet into a new position as a an executive at a luxury retailer. There was a lot going on but I was very excited about everything that was in store for me. I couldn't have been happier . . . I was at the top of my game, until one fateful day in July.

What do you think the odds are of sustaining two brain injuries within 40 days? That's just what happened to me in 2011. I assure you, I wasn't jumping out of airplanes or living in a war zone or playing a professional contact sport . . . I was just like you.

On the afternoon of July 29, 2011, I was going about my typical day as new executive. I was overseeing a staff of 30 cosmetics consultants, over 50 vendors and millions of dollars in product. I was busy to say the least!

I had recently finished a project that had me traveling the world as a global hospitality consultant that took me from Germany to Tahiti and everywhere in between. I was ready to settle down after that year abroad, had returned to Florida, and to my new position.

A few months before, I had met the man of my dreams on a online dating site. He was the tall dark and handsome type that I had been looking for: my own Cary Grant with a wicked sense of humor. While accompanying him on a business trip, overlooking the majesty of the breathtaking Grand Canyon, he had asked me to marry him. I accepted without hesitation. I was overjoyed to think I would be spending the rest of my life with him.

I had been through many experiences at this point in my life that had tested my perseverance and my ability to overcome tough challenges. I had learned from these experiences to choose a mantra that I always told myself in trying times where I seemed knocked down and flat on my back, "Don't Give Up, Get Up!". I also learned about the *art of* visualization. Those two tools became two of the most important things that made a difference in the outcome of any challenging situation I faced. I know that a lot of people speak about positive self-talk or mantras and visualization, but few have elevated it to an effective art form.

The first time I ever heard about the art of positive self talk and visualization was from Jack Canfield in the film *The Secret*. I was glued to the screen when he told his story of how this strategy had worked for him so brilliantly and the success it brought him. I was hooked. But how would I create effective visuals?

I choose to take the knowledge from Mr. Canfield and marry it with my experience in Hollywood. Earlier in my career I had been fortunate to work among some of Hollywood's greatest stars; Bruce Willis, Patrick Swayze, Tom Cruise, Drew Barrymore, Mike Meyers, Elizabeth Taylor and Demi Moore to name a few. The film making community are masters at creating compelling images that seem to pull you into another world. The power of the visual images flickering across the screen can take you on an emotional journey that can literally change the way you look at life, so I decided to create my own "mind movies" with a positive self talk score. Over the years they had been very effective for me in overcoming obstacles.

I had no idea that choosing to make my "mind movies" would become vital to my very survival . . .

That July day in 2011, my life would be forever altered. The events began to unfold as I was making my way to my office after leaving a meeting with the other store executives. Everyone was thrilled with my progress over the short time I had been there. I was riding high with all the accolades and was really feeling at home with my co-workers and staff. I was looking forward to meeting my girlfriend after work to go over wedding ideas and hone in on my dress. That meeting never took place.

Instead, I fell over a cardboard box filled with trash that

someone had left carelessly in a stockrooms walkway. I fell violently forward striking the front of my headfirst on a heavy metal shelf, knocking me unconscious, and then again striking my head as I fell face first onto the concrete floor.

No one knows for sure how long I lay injured on the stockroom floor, but I do know that eventually the paramedics were called. They found me completely unresponsive and still unconscious. Because of my condition they quickly assessed that I would require specialized treatment and they called in the helicopter to transport me to a trauma center an hour away. My fiancée TW was called and they frantically told him that I had been seriously injured and that it was very bad. They advised him to get to the hospital as soon as possible.

Upon awakening the first thing I realized, was that I had a death grip on the side of the stretcher I was laying on. The whole room was spinning and lurching like a carnival ride. My head felt like it was being crushed in a vice and there was an ear-piercing ring in my head. I could barely see and could make out only blurry images because my eyes were tiny slits from the blinding light in the room. There were thundering loud sounds all around me. It sounded like someone turned the volume up to full blast in my ears. My skin was on fire and I had searing pain shooting all over my body. As I struggled to sit up and make sense out of this, I made a terrifying discovery . . . I couldn't move my legs.

I learned later that I had suffered a traumatic brain injury and the blows to my head would effect the functioning of my entire body from then on. I couldn't feel my legs or move them without physically picking them up with special straps like lead weights. I couldn't even sit up because the dizziness and disorientation made me feel ill. My words came out all garbled and slurred. I couldn't recall details, or follow a conversation.

The doctors were not encouraging about my recovery. After all the testing all they could tell us was that we would have to wait and see . . . time MAY make things better. However, they advised, we had to prepare ourselves for no recovery at all. People that had sustained similar trauma were living out their lives in nursing homes unable to function outside of bed, some would just slip into a coma and pass away.

It was then that I knew the only person that was going to be totally responsible for my healing was me and I made a choice to began to work on building my "Mind Movie". I was attempting to use my brain to heal myself but that was the very thing that had been so deeply effected. As much of a challenge as it was, I knew it would be an essential asset to my recovery. However, I was having difficulty building my movie because my brain wasn't cooperating.

My fiancé TW never left my side and kept encouraging me by saying to me over and over again that everything was going to be all right. He told me he believed in me and knew one day I would get up and walk again.

I was literally feeling like I had been beaten all over my body. TW and I joked about feeling like I had been in the ring with Mike Tyson. Then it hit me . . . THAT WAS IT! ROCKY! It was one of my all time favorite movies! I don't know of a person that doesn't want to jump to their feet when they hear the first few bars of the *Rocky* theme song *Gonna Fly Now*.

I worked hard for the next month on my therapy and playing my "mind movie" because at that point I wanted more than anything to go home. Warned I would most likely never be completely free of the vast array of symptoms I suffered, still unable to walk, or care for myself, I was finally released to the full time care of TW. I was still unable to do anything on my own. He would have to bathe me, dress me, feed me, take me to the bathroom and manage all my medications and therapy, all while trying to run his business.

Then I was dealt another devastating blow. One week after being released from my month stay in the rehabilitation hospital, on the way home from a doctors appointment, TW and I were involved in a 40mph collision with a reckless and impaired driver. My side of the vehicle took the brunt of the impact.

I was startled awake with the impact and the airbag exploding in my face. My sunglasses were pushed into my eyes and my head was bouncing around. I began choking on the white chemical from the airbag and couldn't breathe. I had no escape because I couldn't walk.

Unbelievably, still in the infancy of my recovery, I sustained a second traumatic brain injury as my air bag deployed and sent my head into the passenger window. In my condition I was lucky to be alive. Many people die after sustaining a subsequent brain injury while the brain is already damaged.

In the emergency room they determined that not only had I lost all the headway I had made during my rehabilitation, but now I had a host of new injuries. The most serious of the injuries being a second brain injury, but we would discover later: trauma cataracts, that would threaten the complete loss of vision in my left eye. As if that weren't adversity enough to handle, as a result of the car accident: TW was now also seriously injured. He sustained a broken foot and a severe back injury that would later require several surgeries.

The weeks after the car accident were some of the darkest days we have ever faced. The negativity of both of our physical injuries and life circumstances had knocked the wind out of us . . . as if it even hurt to breathe. Our life was full of doctor visits, piles of bills, pain and frustration. Still, I choose to keep on with my "mind movie" and "Don't Give Up, Get Up" mantra.

One day shortly after the car accident, TW said he had an idea. He told me he had an inspiration for a new "mind movie". He said we needed to create our wedding movie and officially set our wedding date. At first I was completely against it. I can even admit to being really angry that he would even suggest such a thing! I told TW we would have to be crazy to set the date! Me wheeling down the isle in a wheelchair in pain, trying to recite garbled words and the great possibility to lose track of what I was doing and make a complete fool out of myself was definitely not what I had in mind for our wedding.

I will never forget TW, gentling taking hold of the armrests of my wheelchair, pulling me close to him and looking me directly in the eye saying in his usual joking manner, "You are going to be Mrs. Walker, so it's kind of important for you get up and get yourself WALKing again quickly. You will walk down that aisle by yourself." Always great at making me laugh, but understanding the seriousness behind the joke, I looked right back into his eyes and it was as if my heart was the one who responded I said "I believe it".

I concentrated many times a day on playing my "mind movie" of my bare foot beach wedding where I would hear over and over "Don't Give Up, Get Up", among the splashing of the waves. I would feel the sand between my toes and the breeze on my face as I imagined myself walking down the isle by myself.

I am proud to say that on April 14, 2012, seven months after sustaining my second brain injury, TW and I were married in a beautiful barefoot beach wedding ceremony. Indeed, I did walk down the isle by myself . . . just as I had heard and seen in my "mind movie" thousands of times before. When you get knocked down like we did, remember Don't Give Up, Get Up!

TAKING 100% RESPONSIBILITY

Jake Ballentine

When you know . . . you know. Even though Caitlin and I were young, I knew she was the one for me. And Caitlin and I both knew that we wanted a family—a big family. Caitlin was one of eight kids and I was one of four. Even as a child, Caitlin's deepest, dearest aspiration had been to be a mother. From age 7 on, if someone asked what she wanted to be when she grew up, Caitlin's reply never varied, "I want to be a mom." And not just a mom, but the best mom.

So after we married in 2009, it wasn't long before we decided to get pregnant. At first when nothing happened, we didn't worry. But after a year of trying, we knew something was wrong. Because of our age—Caitlin was 22 and I was 24—the doctors didn't take our concern seriously. But we insisted on getting tested to find out what the problem was.

The problem turned out to be me. All the tests indicated that our chances of having a child together were slim to none—and I was the one to blame. The doctors didn't offer much hope that my condition could be reversed.

Caitlin tried to be strong—she didn't want me to see her being sad, knowing that would make me feel worse—but I could tell she was struggling as much as I was. For a long time we had no positive answers and no direction at all. It was the darkest period in our lives.

I remember thinking, *Why is this happening to us?* Everywhere we looked, people were getting pregnant. People who didn't want to have kids. People who couldn't care for their kids. People who abandoned their kids. And there we were, ready and willing and aching to have a baby, and we couldn't. It just wasn't fair. I was a big member of the "woe is me" club.

For the next four years, I poured myself into my work, giving motivational talks and using music to inspire junior high and high school students all over the country. I was on the road most of the time. It felt like I was living two lives. On stage I had to be the jovial, happy guy, the inspirational, motivational guy. But that wasn't me off stage. I was miserable. I've never done drugs, I've never been a drinker, so for me, comfort came from food.

I got so depressed that when I was home from the tours, I would sit in front of the television binge-watching Netflix and eating junk food. I'd get calls from people wanting to hire me, and I wouldn't call them back. I felt like a hypocrite talking about having a positive attitude, overcoming obstacles, and going for your dreams, because I wasn't living like that.

One night in late December 2014, sitting on the couch with Caitlin, I hit bottom. Exhausted from traveling and feeling so hopeless about our situation, I began sobbing, asking the same questions I'd been asking for years. "Why was this happening? Why us? Why me?"

For the thousandth time, I heard myself say, "I've done everything I can!" Then, suddenly, like a fish leaping out of the water, a memory popped up. A week or so earlier I'd watched a video of Jack Canfield, one of my personal growth heroes and mentors, talking about taking responsibility for everything in your life. In the video, he speaks with a woman in a live workshop who argues that she's not responsible for getting cancer, and Jack shows her how in many ways, she is. I was struck again by what a difficult principle this is to grasp. Taking responsibility for *everything*?

One second I was crying and the next, I stood up and ran to the bookcase. Finding Jack's book, *The Success Principles*, I grabbed it, turned to the first chapter: "Take 100% Responsibility for Your Life," and began reading. In it, Jack points out that even in situations where it appears we have no control, taking responsibility means looking at the choices we've made so far and accepting that they've contributed to our situation. Then, and most importantly, taking responsibility means making new choices.

Reflecting on this, I knew that what I'd said wasn't true. We'd been seeing doctors, taking tests, trying different vitamins and medications, everything they prescribed. And nothing had worked. But I had NOT done EVERYTHING I could.

You see, early on, after the initial tests, I'd researched male infertility and learned that being overweight is the number one contributor. I'd always struggled with my weight and I had definitely been carrying extra pounds. I'd immediately gone on a diet and like so many times before, I'd failed. Dieting just didn't work for me. Growing up, I had the same diet as my brother, and we did the same activities, but he was skinny. I just thought it was unfair.

Then as time went by and my heart had gotten heavier and heavier, so had I. And in the last few years, I'd stopped caring, mostly because I figured losing the weight was impossible. At that point, I was seventy pounds overweight.

I knew I wasn't eating the food I should be. I was on what I called the "window diet"—most of what I ate came through my car window. But I didn't want to live that way anymore. In that moment, the haze of despair and self-loathing I'd been blinded by for the last four years disappeared, burned off by a white-hot flame of commitment. What could I do to affect this situation?

I made a New Year's resolution to lose the weight. I would make new choices: change my diet and start exercising. I didn't know if I could succeed, but I figured that in the very worst case scenario, I would be able to look back in six months, or a year, or however long it took, and say the words, I *have* done everything I can.

In the beginning. it was slow going. I didn't have the resolve that I have now. Nonetheless, over the next six months, as I started eating better and working out regularly, I lost about 20 pounds. But I still had a long way to go.

That summer, I decided to join Jack Canfield's online Train The Trainer (TTT) program. In that course, you delve more deeply into Jack's principles, applying them more fully in your own life and owning them enough to be able to teach them to others. It was an investment of money, but that was part of the draw for me. I knew that if I made that kind of financial commitment, I'd take it seriously. I wanted more skin in the game. And it worked. Taking TTT definitely turbo-charged my dedication and determination.

In the past, when I tried to make changes, I always put a time limit on my efforts. I'm going to do this and that, and if it doesn't work by this date, forget about it. I'm going back to how I was. But during the training, I began applying one of Jack's Success Principles, "Act As If." From that point on, I "acted as if" I were already that fit, healthy person I wanted to be. It doesn't matter if it takes five years or ten years to completely happen, I'm going to do it, because it's who I am.

By the end of TTT six months later, I'd lost another 35 pounds, a total of 55 pounds! I still have about twenty pounds to lose, but now I feel like I can do anything.

Six years ago, we were told that with my infertility there was nothing more that could be done for us. Now, my key numbers have more than doubled, and we're in the middle of a new fertility treatment. The doctor thinks we'll very likely be pregnant within a few months.

But even if we're not, I can honestly say that my infertility is the best thing that's ever happened to me. A blessing, not a curse. Because of it, I'm healthy, and I feel better than I have in years. Before, I was going to quit my job. I couldn't go hiking, I couldn't play sports, which I'd always loved. Today, Caitlin and I are always on some adventure, hiking in the mountains, going on great trips.

I recently turned 30 and feel like I'm 21. When I turned 29, I felt like I was 40. I've taken responsibility for my life, and there is no better way to live.

IF I WERE BRAVE

Jana Stanfield

The song that put gold and platinum albums on my walls is called "If I Had Only Known." But the song of mine that more people around the world know is "(What Would I Do Today) If I Were Brave?" I co-wrote that song after meeting Jack Canfield and it says a lot about what Jack's work has done for me.

For the last eleven summers, I've been attending Jack's Breakthrough to Success seminar where I get to spend a week with hundreds of other brave difference-makers, asking—and answering —questions like that.

Though I go to perform the music for the event, I actually take the seminar. Every year. *And it's not because I didn't get it the first time.* Going through the program over and over has made the principles that Jack teaches become more deeply ingrained in me. Everything I do, including my songs, has been influenced for the better.

Yet, sometimes, using the Success Principles leads to results that surprise even me. Take for example the orphanage in Bali . . . .

In the winter of 2004, I took a group of people on a Volun-Tour trip to Bali, to experience the culture, and also to do some volunteer work while we were there. We heard of a combination girls' orphanage and foster home, the poorest on the island, and volunteered to go there to do some painting or repair work on their building. As the 50 girls led us through their dilapidated home, we saw that the crumbling walls were too moldy to paint. Above the girls' top bunks, there were thin plastic grocery bags taped to the ceiling to keep rain from dripping through the holes you could see in the roof.

Clearly, this wasn't something a little paint and patching could fix. Right then and there, our group made a commitment: we would each raise $1,000 and pool our money together to rebuild the orphanage. Twenty-eight thousand dollars doesn't sound like a lot, but American dollars go a long way in Bali.

Back home in the states, we all did our best to come up with the funds. However, despite our best efforts, by the time Jack's 2005 BTS seminar rolled around eight months later, we had only raised half of the money we had committed to. We were feeling discouraged that the donations we could gather from family and friends would not be enough to keep the rain off the girls at night. I put it aside to focus on the job I'd been hired to do—provide musical inspiration to the participants in Jack's seminar.

That year the event was being held in Las Vegas. The first morning, as the assistants bustled around getting the room ready for the course, Jack and I stood together on the stage, having our annual 5-minute, bring-me-up-to speed meeting that preceded every seminar. Standing just a few feet away, a group of people waited to meet with Jack individually when he was finished speaking to me. And at any moment, the hundreds of participants who were lining up outside the doors waiting for the seminar to start were going to be flooding into the room.

We wrapped up our conversation and Jack was turning to greet the first person in line when suddenly I had the thought: *I wonder if I could ask for donations for the orphanage from Jack's group?* My heart lifted in sudden hope, and instantly fell. I couldn't ask *that*. Then one of Jack's success principles popped into my mind: *Ask! Ask! Ask!* Followed by: *What would I do today if I were brave?*

I knew I had to take a risk on behalf of the girls. I took a deep breath and before anyone else had a chance to grab Jack's attention, I spoke. "Jack," I said in a halting voice, "I heard about a cell-phone fund-raiser at a seminar where I was a guest speaker recently. If anyone's cell phone went off during the seminar, that person had to give $5 to a charity. What do you think about the idea of having a cell phone fund-raiser this week?"

Jack's response was immediate, "I love that idea! We can give the money to the *Chicken Soup for the Soul Soup Kitchen!*" Then he turned back to face the person who was waiting to meet with him.

Again, I was prompted by the voice in my head: *Jana, what would you do today if you were brave?* I quickly tapped his shoulder and said, "Jack! There's this orphanage in Bali that I'm trying to rebuild for these girls! Can the orphanage be our cell phone charity?"

Jack smiled, "Sure!"

Woo-hoo! I thought.

At the start of the session, Jack made the announcement about the cell phone fundraiser and the orphanage in Bali. As the week went on, the attendees laughed and enjoyed my excited Woo-hoo! every time a cell phone went off.

On the breaks, participants came up to me wanting to make donations to help the girls. A woman contributed $1,000, telling me she tithed to things that fed her spiritually and she felt her experience at the seminar met the criteria. Or in her words, "I have been well fed this week." With each passing day, more people came forward to help. Many participants added $100 to their credit card when they were buying my CDs, saying "Give it to the girls."

One morning I heard a man's voice behind me announce that he had "won big last night"—remember, we were in Las Vegas—and then I felt something being placed inside the pocket of my pants. He said, "Don't turn around. I want to give this money to help the girls at the orphanage *anonymously*." That gave me an idea.

That day I announced from the stage that if people wanted to give anonymously, the big pockets of my International Travel Cargo Pants were accepting donations. For the rest of the week, people kept coming up behind me, filling my pockets with cash. At times, there was so much money being stuffed into those pockets that they literally overflowed.

On the last day of the seminar, a man approached the stage as I was preparing to sing a song. He said that his cell phone had gone off, and that he owed me $5. I thanked him and took the bill he held out. As I was placing the money in my cargo pants pocket, I heard a cell phone go off from somewhere else in the room. I looked up to see who the next donation was coming from, and simultaneously heard another phone ring. And another. And another. Within seconds, the air was filled with the din of hundreds of electronic ringtones. I looked around in wonder. Everyone in the room was laughing and smiling as they held their ringing cell phones in the air. Then, en masse, the group stood up and, eyes sparkling with joyful mischief, began digging money from their purses and wallets and filling the aisles, making their way to the front of the room. They made a big pile of money in the middle of the stage as I watched open-mouthed.

I was in awe. *Hundreds* of attendees had somehow organized this idea of helping the girls, while simultaneously managing to keep it a secret from me.

And they weren't finished.

The giving continued as a woman in the back stood up and made an announcement: whatever the total amount of the pile on the stage, she was willing to double it! Then a man jumped up from his seat and matched her pledge. I knelt by the mound of bills on the stage and sobbed with gratitude. I was so deeply touched.

That week in Las Vegas, we raised $15,000!—just what was needed to rebuild what is now a beautiful, new orphanage for the girls in Bali, with strong white walls and a roof that keeps them dry during the rainy season.

I never imagined that a change in the girls' living conditions would have such a huge impact on their self-esteem. I believe the love and caring from all of those people at the seminar was somehow imbued into the actual building materials of the new orphanage—and then transferred to the girls inside. I like to think that they are living in a structure made from love. When I see those girls now, every year when I go back, I see as much of a transformation in them as in the leaking, moldy building they once occupied.

Miracles are there for the asking, if we're brave enough to ask.

What would *you* do today if *you* were brave?

PROUDLY FILIPINO

Penny Bongato

"What am I doing here?" I asked myself, on the first day of Jack Canfield's 2014 Breakthrough to Success (BTS) Workshop in Scottsdale, Arizona. Here I was, with my son, surrounded by 300 more people. *Why am I even holding the microphone and ready to speak?*

On the first day, Jack asked the participants if anyone would like to share something with the group. There were a few volunteers and in my mind, they were "whites." And then all of a sudden, I felt *my* hand raising.

What? Is this really me volunteering to speak? "Hi, I am Penny from the Philippines. The Philippines, for those who don't know, is a small country in Asia. Being here in front of you all is scary for me. Being around white people scares me more. I belong to the brown race. But I am here to learn and conquer my fears." I spoke! I really did! I couldn't believe what I did.

The participants and Jack clapped and immediately I felt welcomed. When the others spoke, I realize that each one of us have our own fears and beliefs. It may be the color of our skin, our childhood, parents, family, being bullied in school, alcohol, drugs—whatever they may be, everyone had something to share.

How did I ever come to attend Breakthrough to Success? Before 2014 I could never have imagined it.

My love for my race and country really started in 2003, when I started an amazing career in one of the sunshine industries of the Philippines—the Business Process Outsourcing (BPO) industry. Contact centers were starting to grow in the Philippines then, with most of the clients coming from the U.S. I was interviewed by two American executives from Cincinnati. Jim Watson, the HR executive handed me a job offer, to be employee number 1 of one of the biggest contact centers in the U.S.— Convergys. Director of Human Resources for this big multinational company which will just be starting in the Philippines.

Wow! What an honor! I grabbed the opportunity. What is the work? For me, it was joining a start up company. Being number 1. And I was giving jobs to Filipinos. Filipinos don't have to only work as domestic helpers in Singapore or in Hong Kong or in the Middle East. Opportunities are here, in the Philippines! I just love it!

What I loved most about my work though is having to present to clients what the Filipinos can do—our ability to speak the English language well, our love for others, our innate orientation to be of service to others and most of all, our hospitality and compassion for others. My work allowed me to hone my presentation and speaking skills, and deal with executives from different companies. What more could I ask? The compensation was extremely good, the exposure to meet executives from overseas, and I was making my name known.

The job, however, was not without challenges—having to work the night shift, managing chaotic growth, meeting the numbers. And most of all, office politics. I found myself questioning even my own capabilities. Can I really do this job? Is it something that I want to do?

But there was no time to think. I have four children, all in school. My husband is retired. So much dependent on me, so I thought, *I cannot fail. I cannot fail. I cannot fail.* Those words kept on entering my mind. *I have a family to feed, children to raise.* My mind said, *Make it work.* I needed the money.

In the midst of having fame, money and name in the industry, I wasn't happy. After 8 years of working in the sunshine industry, I decided to resign and quit my job. Did I have a back-up plan? No, I didn't. One day, I was suddenly jobless. All I knew was that I have the faith and I believe that every setback is an opportunity for a greater comeback.

While in the state of discerning what to do next in my life, I came across to the book *The Power of Focus* by Jack Canfield, and

I started applying everything being said in the book. I started writing goals in the different areas of my life—career, financial, personal, and vacations. I even started collecting pictures that represented my future dreams and even photos of my past successes.

"What are you doing, Ma?" My daughter, Mikee, asked. "I am compiling photos of my successes so that when I feel down, I can just look at these photos and know that I had these accomplishments." When I was looking at the photos of my past accomplishments, I heard a voice in my head say, *Past accomplishments. You can't do them again. You are done!* All these limiting beliefs, these negative thoughts never seemed to stop. The past is past. You need to think of today and tomorrow. But how?

Then I saw an ad in the newspaper. "Jack Canfield is coming to Manila on September 27, 2010 at the SMX Convention Center," the headline said. I immediately grabbed this opportunity to see Jack in person in Manila.

Meeting Jack live and hearing the Success Principles directly from him was a totally different experience. I knew I was on the right track with setting goals, cutting out pictures, and visualizing. After the seminar, I was of course, one of many who approached Jack, asked for his autograph and promised myself I would do what I learned in that workshop. I even decided to take a new job—teaching in College and working for an association of BPO companies—once again continuing to help the industry grow and flourish in the country. Proud of what the Filipinos can do. I was religiously doing what I learned at the workshop but like most things, I was doing it religiously after the workshop, but being consistent in living the principles was, in all honestly, difficult.

In 2014, since I was now on Jack's mailing list, I read the announcement of the August Breakthrough to Success. *I will attend, I told myself. I will have the courage to do this. I can do it!* It was scary at first, but I am a Filipino, I can do it.

I conquered my fear, having volunteered to speak on the first day of BTS. *I will not feel ashamed of my race. I will not be intimidated by these tall white men. I will not be the little quiet Penny who always has this question "Can I do it? Am I good enough?"*

Five full days with Jack at the incredible Breakthrough to Success training changed my thinking. The first principle was "Take 100% Responsibility for Your Life and Your Results. Stop blaming and complaining." I knew I was doing that already. I know I have a positive attitude and I almost always initiate and volunteer.

What struck me most in the workshop was the principle "Be Clear Why You Are Here." What is your life purpose? I was definitely struggling with the exercises on life purpose. Even during the guided visualization part, nothing came to my mind. *Why am I here? What are my qualities? What am I good at? What do I enjoy doing?* These things for sure: I love teaching. I love presenting. I love giving jobs to the Filipinos. I love being able to help the country grow. I love to give hope to Filipinos who think there are no other options but to work abroad. I love to be able to inspire my students to be what they want to be. The AHA moment came when I actually realized what my purpose is: *to inspire as many Filipinos to become the best that they can be before I expire.*

Learning the other principles, working with different groups, and meeting different people from different countries were all valuable, but what I valued most in BTS was meeting new friends who truly understood what we were all going through—especially Charlie Collins and Forrest Willett who had great stories to tell about the challenges they were faced with and how they had overcome those challenges. We were speaking the same language. *If they can do it,* I thought, *so can I!* I can do anything I set my mind to.

The last day of BTS, Jack discussed his Train the Trainer program and his vision of having one million trainers teaching the success principles by 2030. I immediately thought, *I want to be one of them. I want to be able to help the Filipinos reach their dreams, be the best they can be, not second class citizens, but for us to be proud of what we are.* But my inner voice also said, *Yeah, right. But I can't afford it.* But as we had learned in the training, "Just focus on and commit to the What, and the How will show up."

I was focused on signing up for the Train the Trainer (TTT) Program. I didn't know how I'd do it, but I put it in my vision board—to be a Certified Canfield Trainer in the Success Principles. "Commit to the What, and the How will show up."

However, In September 2014, only a month after BTS, our doctor delivered the most disturbing news—my husband was diagnosed with colon cancer. Besides the expense, there was no way that I could now even think of attending TTT. I wanted to focus on my husband. Chemotherapy or TTT expenses? Of course, my husband was my priority.

Yet my dream of joining the Train the Trainer program was still there. "Just focus on the What. The How will show up." And guess what? The How did show up! I attended the TTT in February 2015, and my husband came along for the vacation. Where did the money come from? I really don't know; it just showed up. And what an experience TTT was! And my husband and I had our vacation in Las Vegas (our first time to visit Las Vegas). Spending every moment available creating happy memories with my husband was also one of my goals.

After the February TTT week came the June pre-certification week, and I was again preparing for that. Then another unfortunate event came about. In April, my husband was diagnosed with prostate cancer. Oh no! What will I do now? I was asking, "Why Lord? Why the second time?"

"Don't let my illness stop you from achieving your dreams. Go! I will always be here to support you," my husband whispered to me. He had to undergo treatment once again, and after the treatment, he said, "Don't postpone anymore. Go and I'll join you."

So many thoughts rushed through my mind. *I don't have this high paying job anymore. Where will I get the money? Will his health be able to take the travel? Is it too risky? What if I just postpone it?*

But there we were in Arizona again in June. My thoughts were, *TTT, here I come. I am ready.* And, *Here we (my husband and I) are, creating memories again.*

Day 1 on the TTT preparation week, Jack asked for three volunteers to lead meditations on days 3, 4 and 5; and 1 to do the presentation in the afternoon of Day 1. Jack said, "There are index cards on your table. Those who wish to volunteer, please write your name on the card and place it in the appropriate box—one box for the meditation and one box for the presentation."

Will I volunteer? I asked myself. Hahaha! The immediate answer was, *No way! I don't need the stress.* I saw some of the other participants writing their names and dropping the cards in the appropriate box. When Jack said it was time for a break, I took a look at how many cards were in the box for the first presentation. I thought to myself, *If I volunteer, my chances of being called is less than 10%.* And then suddenly, I remembered my goal—to be a Certified Canfield Trainer in the Success Principles. I want to be an international speaker speaking in 20 countries. And then I remembered the other principles—Take Action and Lean Into It. So, I wrote my name and dropped the card in the box.

After the break Jack picked three names for the meditation and announced each one. Then he picked one for the presentation, and said, "The one who will present this afternoon is . . . Penny Bongato."

Wait!! Did I just hear my name? Am I dreaming? Why did I even volunteer in the first place? Can I take it back? Please???

My name was called. My name? I will not be scared . . . but who was I kidding? I was terrified!!! Penny to be the first presenter in the whole program! Me! The small Filipina who said in the first BTS that speaking in a group of white people scares me. I had to face the challenge. This is IT!

While Jack was conducting the training, I couldn't concentrate anymore. I was thinking, *What if I make a fool of myself? What if I stutter? What if I shake? What if . . . .* And then I started thinking something else. *I will do good. I practiced. I know my presentation and I will get feedback* (Another key success principle is Use Feedback to Your Advantage).

The time came when Jack called me to present. 15 minutes. I went on stage, talked to Jack for a few seconds, tried to loosen up (with difficulty), and started speaking. I felt my whole body was shaking. I could hardly breathe. *Is this really happening?* As I began my presentation I began to relax and I knew, I can do this. And I felt that this is where I belong. I really, really love the principles and I love talking about them and teaching them. I felt then and I still feel now that I can do this forever!

Well, I did receive feedback—from Kathleen Seeley, Patty Aubery and Jack Canfield. Feedback I wouldn't have gotten if I hadn't volunteered. Someone later told me, "You are so lucky. You just got $25,000 worth of feedback from Jack!" Oh yes, I did it!

In August 2015, I received my certification as a Canfield Certified Trainer in the Success Principles and just this month, April 2016, I became a Certified Trainer in the Canfield Methodology. I have already conducted numerous trainings on the Success Principles, for students, and professionals, in the Philippines and even in Singapore. I talk about the principles almost all the time. But the best part, I know that I am living the principles myself.

I have written new goals. I changed my vision board twice already. I meditate and do my affirmations daily. I still have my accountability partner, who I have talked to every week for the past eight months already. There are times that I feel I do slide back and have those negative thoughts again, but having my partner keeps me in check. I am truly grateful for all that made this happen and for all the wonderful experiences I am having.

Another dream is also coming true—four of us from the Train the Trainer group, Forrest Willet, Marco Aguilar, Danny Khursigara together with Serely Alcaraz, of the ITD Consulting Group will be conducting our first international workshop in the Philippines (in Manila and Cebu). It all started with a goal, and it will happen in July 2016.

Oh, and my dream to be an international speaker in 20 countries—I have already spoken in seven—the Netherlands, Singapore, India, South Africa, Colombia, Indonesia and the Philippines. I continue to pursue my dream while helping others pursue theirs.

Every morning, the moment I wake up each day, I begin to give new life to my dreams by speaking words of affirmation, faith and victory. I make decisions that are aligned with what I truly want, and I pursue my passion to help others, particularly the Filipinos, be the best that we can be.

I am Penny Bongato, Filipino, the first Canfield Certified Trainer in the Success Principles in the Philippines and in Asia. Truly proud to be Pinoy.

WHY ARE YOU HERE?

Gerry Visca

My mother was a fashion designer who had studied in Italy and could design the most incredible wedding dresses. As a kid, I'd watch her work. One day, as she sat at her drawing table, I noticed her close her eyes and sit motionless for a few minutes.

"What are you doing?" I asked.

Opening her eyes and smiling at me, she said, "I'm visualizing what this dress is going to look like." Then she sketched what she'd seen. When she finished, she said, "I want you to try that too. Before you start to do something, picture in your mind what you want to accomplish."

I was around 11 or 12 years old at the time. A couple of years earlier, my mom had taken my two brothers and me away from our abusive father to raise us on her own. We didn't have much money, but she poured her energy into us, shining a light on us and telling us we could do anything we set our minds to. That day, though I didn't completely understand it at the time, she was teaching me to visualize my future.

After that, I began picturing things I wanted: what it would be like to win my next tennis tournament—I was big into tennis at the time—or what it would be like to get an A on an important school exam. I'd still practice and study, of course, but this picturing seemed to give me an extra boost. I'd always been very visual, but I give credit to my mother for showing me how to direct that talent, teaching me what I would later learn was a proven tool for achieving success.

In college, I studied architecture. Given my visual skills, that felt like a natural choice for me. But architecture isn't just about buildings; it's also about understanding the essence of things. As I continued my studies, I learned I also had a talent for perceiving this deeper aspect of design. This came in handy while working as an intern architect—I found I was good at presenting projects to people, getting them to embrace and even feel inspired by the firm's vision for their building, even when they'd initially been against what we were proposing.

But it soon became clear to me that architecture wasn't my true calling. At first I didn't know what I wanted to do. I just knew I needed to do something different. With that desire, I launched a business focused on what I called "transformative branding." Basically, I used that idea from architecture about finding the "essence of something" and helped companies find their "brand essence." That was in 1999, when "branding" was still a new concept.

Fast-forward eight years . . . The business was a huge success. I'd married and my wife worked with me as a full partner, and our staff had expanded to fifteen employees. We served thousands of clients, including a number of well-known international corporations. In the space of just eight years, we'd achieved everything we'd envisioned for the company.

And yet—I was miserable.

The firm had gotten too big, becoming an administrative nightmare. We had two offices, and I was constantly rushing back and forth between them. We were also launching new software, and I was writing my first book. On top of all that, my wife and I both knew we weren't happy in our marriage.

Discomfort can be one of the most powerful catalysts for growth. Although I had plenty of discomfort, I had no idea what kind of growth might possibly come out of that. I had an inkling that it had something to do with inspiring people, but I didn't know what that meant. I just knew I craved something other than what I'd already achieved.

One day, my wife gave me a set of CDs as a gift, saying she knew I was in a transition and that she sensed there was something big waiting for me. We'd both been exposed to some great books and

CDs about personal growth through some training she'd had as a life coach, but this was different. I glanced at the title, *The Success Principles*, and the photo of the author, Jack Canfield. Looking at Jack's face, I had a deep sense that I'd seen him before, and I had visions—a strong kind of intuition—that we would have some connection to each other later on. I didn't understand any of this, but the next day, driving to a networking convention, I cleared away all my other CDs and popped in the first disc of *The Success Principles*.

As soon as I heard Jack's voice, I knew that this was something different. It was special in a way I couldn't quite understand. As I continued to listen, the meaning of his words moved me profoundly. At one point I was so overwhelmed, I had to stop the car on the side of the road. This sounds funny—but I felt so much expansion that it was almost difficult to breathe deeply enough. At the same time, energy pulsated through my body in a feeling of euphoria. I just accepted that and let it flow through me, because I knew that something amazing was about to happen, that a life-changing transformation was about to kick in. When I arrived at my destination, I truly felt like a different person. As the day progressed, I noticed that I was giving ten times more of myself than I'd ever given at an event like that. It was as if I were super-charged!

For the next three months, I immersed myself in *The Success Principles*. I'd wake up and start listening to the CDs, I'd listen to them throughout the day, and then I'd fall asleep the same way. I listened to those CDs over and over again that I could almost finish Jack's sentences. I owned that material and I let it guide me.

At the end of that three-month period, a fully formed vision appeared in my head. I knew exactly what I needed to do. For my business, that meant a complete reorganization. But for me, personally, it meant finally acting on the words that had first made me pull my car to the side of the road: Take 100% responsibility for your life, and be clear why you're here.

Being clear about my purpose came first for me. I knew that I could no longer continue to do what I'd been so successful at—helping companies identify their brand. I needed to do more than that. I needed to help individuals find their life purpose and be inspired to action through that discovery. That purpose rang true in every cell of my body!

Taking responsibility for my life was trickier. I was already an extremely responsible person. In fact, as the driving energy behind the success of my business, I felt as though I was responsible not only for my life, but also for everyone else's lives. I was getting projects for my employees, making sure they could pay their bills, and on top of that, trying to keep my wife happy. I never had the feeling of taking responsibility for what I really wanted. What did I want to create? Who did I want to be? The changes I needed to make, in order to live my life's purpose, amounted to allowing my employees to take the same kind of responsibility for their lives that I wanted to take for mine.

Keeping the vision that had come to me in my mind and referring to it often, I launched into action like a massive explosion. First, I saw that I needed to pare down our operations, focusing on the quality of our clients, rather than the quantity. This meant letting some people go. Next, I threw myself into transforming the branding process into a full-day workshop that incorporated the Success Principles.

This explosion shook everything up. I was no longer Gerry the Creative Director, responsible for providing projects for everyone. This was a big shock. My wife, especially, resisted the changes that Jack inspired in me, even though she'd been the one who had given me those CDs. She told me that she felt she'd created a monster. She was used to our level of financial success and defined herself by the work that she did.

Ultimately, when the smoke cleared, I saw that the "reorganization" was the best thing that could have happened for everyone involved. Several of my staff left to create their own successful branding company, something they wouldn't have done if things had remained as they were. And after my wife and I divorced, she began working in a completely different field, one that suited her well. I'm grateful to her for leading me to Jack, and to him for showing me how to get clear on the reason why I'm here.

Today, as one of Canada's top motivational speakers, I live that purpose, inspiring other people—through my books and coaching and speaking engagements—to take 100% responsibility for their lives and to commit to "living their WHY" (which I define as the "World Helped by You"). It's part of my WHY to teach my clients Jack's work, including visualization, the success principle I first learned at my mother's knee.

In the past few years, I've helped change the lives of thousands of people all over the world. And we're all ignited by the same flame—the one Jack passed to us in the form of a torch called *The Success Principles*.

SCHOOLED FOR SUCCESS

JoAnn Myers

It was 1997. As I scanned the shelves of books at the Columbus, Georgia public library, a title jumped out at me: *The Aladdin Factor* by Jack Canfield and Mark Victor Hansen.

Hmmm, I thought, *I could sure use a genie right about now*. I was a substitute teacher at the time, moving around a lot due to my husband's career, and unsure of what the future held for me. What I was sure of was that I wasn't where I really wanted to be.

I checked the book out of the library, took it home, and read it. It was one of those "a-ha-change-your-life" experiences! I learned that the first step in *getting* what you want is *knowing* what you want. As I read page after page, it became clear to me that my passion was to help people in a big way through education. Motivated by this vision, I decided to get my Master's Degree and applied for a graduate program in school psychology at Georgia State University.

I didn't get in.

The program had about 500 applicants for 20 seats. In the past, I would have given up. But because I had learned the "Ask, Ask, Ask," principle from Jack's book, I kept checking back at the school, telling them I was interested and asking to see if somebody had dropped the course. Two days before the program started, I received a call that they had an open spot. Thank you, Aladdin!

After completing my degree, I used the Ask, Ask, Ask principle many times to find teaching positions. Eventually, in 2005, I landed my first job as a principal.

By this time, I'd moved to Albuquerque, New Mexico, and the school I was in charge of was a maximum-security facility for incarcerated juveniles. Working with those kids was an eye-opener for me. During our intake interviews with my students, I'd do a life action plan with them and ask, "What do you want to do with your life? What are your goals? Your dreams?"

Nine times out of ten, the incoming student would look at me blankly, with no idea what I was talking about. These were essentially good kids—some of them even brilliant—who'd hit a road-block in their lives, but what truly broke my heart was that they had lost sight of any goals they may have once had.

It was then I realized: if I really wanted to help kids, it went beyond just providing a good, quality education. I had to teach them how to set goals and dream—and then how to make those goals and dreams come true.

Getting through to those kids wasn't going to be easy. They were suspicious of authority and my appearance didn't help the situation. I've been described as a petite, blond Barbie-doll. When people meet me, they often think I grew up as a little rich girl with a silver spoon in my mouth, and that whatever I wanted came easily to me. I know the kids I worked with, Hispanic, African American, Native American, took one look at me and thought the very same thing.

But that couldn't have been further from the truth. I grew up in poverty, on food stamps and public assistance, with an abusive father. When I went to a college, I was the poor kid. The teachers didn't believe in me and no one was rooting for me. But something inside me knew that I was capable of more than people believed I was.

I tried to explain to my students that I wasn't that different from them, but they remained skeptical. How could I help them see that they were also more capable than the world believed? That it was what was inside that counted?

Once again, I found myself at the public library, face-to-face with another of Jack Canfield's books. I recognized Jack's name on the cover of The Success Principles. Although it was a thick book, once I picked it up, I couldn't put it down. After putting the kids to bed at nine o'clock, I'd read till the wee hours of the morning. I read that book from cover to cover in three days.

Then, I read it again and this time, I did every single activity that Jack outlines in it. I wrote goals for every area of my life, put them in a big flip binder and on index cards, and read them every day. I introduced *The Success Principles* to a couple of co-workers and we had a weekly book study meeting to work on the principles.

In the book, Jack recommends that you set a goal that is really hard to reach—a breakthrough goal. Mine was for the kids at the juvenile justice facility to have an athletic team. I feel strongly that we can't treat incarcerated kids like criminals and then expect them to integrate back into society in one, two, or three years. We have to give them a place where they can be treated as normal kids, and I thought sports would be a great way to go about it.

So, despite the pushback we knew we'd receive, we put our request out there: Let our kids form a team that can play with the other teams in the area. That was a huge step for us. It was a goal that brought up those roadblocks Jack talks about—the ones where you have to go over, under, and through. I can't tell you how many times we were told, "No, you can't do that." But we wouldn't accept no for an answer. We just kept working and working until we made it happen. Finally, after two years, we were able to establish a track team that could participate with the local public schools.

Now our students, who had been involved in gang violence were participating in sports activities, doing relay races and passing the baton at track meets—right alongside the other "normal" kids. This caused a major shift in how they viewed themselves.

Jack's work continued to guide me to go outside of the box with my students. I started using *The Success Principles* language with them: "We aren't taking no for an answer! Reject rejection! Ask, Ask, Ask! Take 100% responsibility for yourself."

Whenever they began to point the finger and make excuses, I'd remind them: "As long as you're going to blame others, you can't take control of your life." I really saw the need for teaching the kids to stay in touch with a bigger picture.

As a result, our students maintained a good attitude. Even in the freezing cold and in the pouring rain, when the track was a river of mud, those kids wanted to practice. They didn't want to let the school down.

In another attempt to show these kids what was possible for them, we started a program taking them to college campuses around the state. I can't tell you how many hoops I had to jump through to get permission to do that. And what I heard from our kids on the bus coming back to the facility was "Those kids look like us, they talk like us, and dress like us!" After those college visits, the motivation the kids felt was tangible.

Using Jack's principles was not only changing my life but the lives of the students I worked with. We even had one student get a full, 4-year scholarship in engineering to New Mexico State in Las Cruces. He was leaving our facility and had a few classes he needed to complete to graduate. Though it required going through a million different channels—connecting with people that I knew would support me and who could think outside the box too—we were able to list him as our valedictorian and he was able to graduate. He is doing fabulously now.

In 2008, I went to Miami for spring break. I took *The Success Principles* with me to read again, as I'm constantly revisiting my goals. On that trip, I made the decision to take my passion for changing the world through education to the next level: I would open my own charter school—in *New York City*.

By that time, things were on an even keel in New Mexico. The programs we'd put in place were producing great results in the students and I was ready for another challenge. And since I'd always had a fantasy about opening a charter school in New York City, I decided to go for it.

A charter school is an independent publically-funded school that has the freedom to be more innovative and adapt to the unique educational needs of its students. It requires a lengthy application process.

I enlisted a woman I knew to work with me as assistant principal and the two of us began composing our charter. Because we were including Jack's principles as part of our charter, we thought it would be a good idea to attend Jack's Breakthrough to Success conference that summer.

The conference was all that I had hoped it would be, and more. Not only did I get to meet Jack Canfield in person, but I also found myself surrounded by hundreds of positive, success-minded people and immersed in all the material I'd been studying for so many years.

At one point during the conference, we had an assignment to write our goals and then come up with affirmations based on those goals. One of the affirmation statements my friend and I wrote was, *"We will open a high-performing charter school in New York City by September 2011,"* and we would read it every day.

This affirmation worked so well that our goal came true a couple of years before it was supposed to happen! The very next year we opened a charter school in the Bronx. We called it Equality Charter School, because of our belief in equal access to high-quality education for all students. Working in a school that I had so carefully and consciously created was an amazing experience and I learned a lot from it—both what worked and what didn't.

After a couple of years in New York, I found that the idea of living in the city was more fun than actually living there, so I decided to move back to Albuquerque. Poised to soar to the next level in my life, I read *The Success Principles* again. This reading inspired me to commit to opening a school where *The Success Principles* were the basis of our charter.

Again, I found a partner to help me build my vision and the two of us read and worked with a different chapter of *The Success Principles* each week. We even started a blog about it. For months, we lived and breathed that charter school application, which ended up being almost a 300-page document. We submitted it and waited.

As you can imagine, the competition is fierce. I believe that as a result of our immersion into the principles, we were able to manifest that rare event: approval for a brand new charter school in Albuquerque! Our school, called Mission Achievement and Success, is unique. Because I truly believe in the power of *The*

Success Principles, we wrote an entire curriculum to go with it. It's a mandatory course for graduation.

I wish that I had studied *The Success Principles* when I was in school. Growing up, I was fearful, hesitant to act on my ideas and goals. But after reading the book so many times, I've internalized the principles. All the qualities I need to succeed—direction, clarity, and confidence—which were always there, have been unburied in me and are readily available.

Jack says if you're living your life purpose, your work should be fun. I love what I do, so I know I'm on track there. But my true gauge of success is that I can sleep at night, happy with the decisions I make each day that positively affect my students' lives—and the lives of their families. Learning the principles that have been the bedrock of their achievements, and mine, was the most important education I ever got.

SERVING THE WORLD

Kate Butler

At 27-years-old, I was diagnosed with a heart condition. By the time it was detected, the condition was so severe that all the testing, result appointments and consultations that usually take years, all happened for me in a matter of weeks. I knew by the sense of urgency that something was severely wrong. My doctors told me my heart was beating too fast and unless they operated to burn off these overactive valves in my heart, that one of these times in the near future my heart would beat too strongly and burst, causing me to drop dead on the spot. Could you imagine receiving this news at 27-years-old? I was in shock. I was terrified. I was devastated.

I listened to the diagnosis. I followed the doctors' instructions. I went through the motions of surgery to correct my broken heart. However, I knew something they didn't. I knew that my heart had a message for me. I knew that my heart was communicating with me this way to get my attention. I innately knew that my heart was giving me a wake up call. But it would be three more years before I would really listen.

Here I was, the mom of two kids under three. I had a college education, a highly successful corporate career under my belt, a loving husband, two beautiful little girls, a gorgeous home . . . and yet, here I was standing in the middle of the nursery, looking around, asking myself, *Is this it? Is this where your journey ends? Is this what your life is going to be?* That voice actually brought me to my knees that day. I was watching my beautiful daughter nap and her essence and light were igniting a fire in my belly. I started to get these flashes of my children and their remarkable spirits and talents. They were so extraordinary and thinking of their life, I wanted to create more, serve more, be more . . . be better for them. The thoughts were vivid. They were clear. They were powerful. So powerful, that in that moment, I had no choice but to surrender.

Once I surrendered to the voice, I asked, *Where do I begin?* And like magic, I began noticing little miracles each day that were pointing me in the right direction. One of those miracles showed up in the way of an email inviting me to a seminar teaching *The Success Principles*. At first glance, it did not strike me as something I needed. I thought to myself, I don't need to learn about success. I thought I had that part under control. I was making six figures by the time I was 25 years old. I had managed multiple offices, multiple teams, multiples streams of revenue. Success? I had that down. But then the voice came back, *Where are you now? What is your purpose?* In that moment, I was struck with the same feelings, the same *knowing*, that I had the moment I was diagnosed with my heart condition. My heart was trying to tell me something again. I would later know this to be my "heart story." This time I was ready to listen.

I looked around. I had started my own company about two years ago. And although we turned a profit each year, my actual take home pay was nothing to brag about. I certainly was not making six figures any longer. But it was more than that. I no longer enjoyed what I was doing with this company. The work no longer lit me up inside. I did not believe that this was my purpose on this earth. There had to be more.

Being guided by my heart story, I read further into the email. This seminar promised clarity of my vision, identifying my purpose, and the tools to start a business based on my true passion. Now this was speaking to me. I immediately registered.

When I got to the seminar, I still was not quite sure what I was doing there, but I was trusting my heart. I had an idea for a children's book, but no idea how to go about publishing it. I was not really in touch with my passion to know what sort of business to start next. I was very unclear of my path, but the one thing I knew is that I was here to do more. I knew I had a purpose. I also knew that in order for me to be the best wife and mother I could be, I owed it to my family to be the best version of me I could be.

The week I spent learning Jack Canfield's Success Principles transformed my entire life. I immediately began implementing the principles. The first thing I did was take 100% responsibility for my life. I took inventory of the good things in my life and gave myself credit. I took inventory of the things I wasn't happy with in my life and I took responsibility. This decision changed everything. It was so empowering. I choose to stop putting the blame on my husband for not having enough money for all the extras in life. I stopped complaining about how unfair it was that I was in debt and how I could never catch a break. My new reality was that if I wanted more money, I could choose to create more money. I choose to stop blaming being overweight on my pregnancies, having young children, not having enough time and not having enough help. The new reality was that I would either make time for the gym or not, but it was my choice and my choice alone. I made a decision that it was not my husband's job or my family's job or my friend's job to make me happy. If I was not in a good mood, or if I was not happy with my life, I had the power to change it by choosing to be happy. It was up to me! When I stopped blaming others for the circumstances in my life, I realized that I had the power. The choice was mine! I felt free. I was no longer a victim of circumstances and I stood in my power for the first time in years.

Once I became clear on what I wanted and set specific goals, I applied the Rule of 5* to help get focused. This principle is a straight up game changer! When I first began implementing the Rule of 5, I could not understand how it was much different than my "To-Do" list that was already three pages. Not long into my practice, I realized why this principle is so profoundly effective. It became crystal clear that a majority of things on my "To-Do" list were about other people. It was full of what they needed from me, rather than a

---

* The Rule of 5 is Principle #23 in *The Success Principles* by Jack Canfield. It is the commitment to take 5 action steps that will move you toward the completion of your most important goal every day.

list moving towards my goals. As I began to apply this principle, my list would begin to reflect things like, "research illustrators" or "spend 30 minutes on developing the book launch campaign." Things like this had never made my list before. I wanted to publish a children's book, but I had no idea where to start. I would always tell myself that I would get to it when I had the time. The problem was, I never had the time. I was too busy working on my "To-Do" list. The Rule of 5 gave me an opportunity to step outside of the routine I was accustomed to and re-think how I wanted to spend my time and where I wanted to focus my energy. This daily practice revolutionized my success.

It's funny. For years I defined success as the number of zeros in my bank account or the title on my business card. By those standards, I was successful. What I couldn't figure out was why I wasn't happy. Through my work with Jack, I learned one simple statement that brought everything full circle. Jack said to me, "It is not about the money. Find a way to serve and you will be truly wealthy." I did just that. I connected to my passion, and from that place I began writing books and started coaching to serve and inspire others. Once my paradigm around success shifted, it was all so effortless. The clients, the sales, and the money . . . it was all flowing so easily. Previously, I had always tried to force it, always trying so hard to make more or get to the next level. Now, here I was in a job that truly fulfilled me. And even though I had many more zeros in my bank account, that was no longer what was driving me. I was now coming from a place of clear intention. I wanted to bring my gifts to the world in a way of service to help others. It was time for my "heart story" to serve the world.

In the span of two years, I went from an overworked, stressed out, high anxiety, work-from-home mom to a #1 Best Selling Children's Author and highly sought after Mindset Coach who is calm, peaceful, *present* and happy.

The success of my new business was tremendous. My first book, *More than Mud*, was an Amazon best seller for over 70 weeks straight, and still counting. My second book, *More than Magic*, became a #1 best seller on Amazon before the book even released and has remained on the best seller charts ever since. I built a successful and lucrative coaching business, which allows me to travel the world with my family while inspiring others to connect with their heart story.

My income has more than tripled in the last year. But the real success was this: I became clear on my vision. I now know my purpose. I am serving the world with my unique heart story. I am more present with my husband and children. Our family is happier. I am now fulfilled and making a difference doing what I love. This is the true success.

When you are truly serving your heart story, the possibilities are endless. All of our hearts are here with a message. It is our duty and our service to listen to our heart story and serve in the way that only we are here to serve.

A DREAM (HOME) COME TRUE

Daniel Hunter

For years, I've been living my life using universal principles like the ones in Wallace Wattles' book, *The Science of Getting Rich*, Napoleon Hill's *Think and Grow Rich*, and Og Mandino's books. As a salesperson, I've found them immensely helpful.

So when I saw the film *The Secret* in 2007, it wasn't new material for me, but what did stand out was Jack Canfield's explanation of the Law of Attraction. Listening, I understood at a new level the power of our intentions, goals, and our focus—both professionally and personally. This really became clear when I set out to find my dream home.

In June of 2011, my family and I rented a house in a beautiful neighborhood on Maui. For about a year, we scoured the area looking for a home to buy. We drove up and down every street within a 10-mile radius, but couldn't find anything that was right—the ones we could afford, we didn't like, and the ones we liked, we couldn't afford. The neighborhood we were renting in was exactly where we wanted to live, but it was clear there was nothing in our price range.

Then in February of 2012, we heard from a friend that a house down the street from our rental home, which was owned by her uncle, was going into foreclosure. I was familiar with the house and was thrilled. It was perfect! We knew this was our one chance to get into the neighborhood.

When it came on the market a few months later, I immediately put in an offer that I knew was low, but I felt it was worth a try. It turned out to be the lowest offer the bank received and they refused it. They didn't even counter.

For the next week, I kept a close watch on the house for signs that it had been sold, but nothing happened. Three weeks went by and I got a call from a man at the bank named Carlos telling me that they were lowering the price of the house. This time I got serious. I ran the numbers, forward and backward, and came up with a price I could truly afford: $780,000. Though it was significantly lower than the asking price, it was a stretch for our finances. Still I felt it was the right price. When I submitted the offer, I told Carlos, "This is it. All my cards are on the table. No games."

Again, the bank didn't counter since they received an offer of $979,000. We'd lost it. I told my wife Julie, "Yeah, that was a long shot. I'm not surprised we didn't get it."

Julie, who knew the principles I'd been studying, gave me a strange look and said, "Why do you say that? You know as well as I do that we need to be clear about what we want and expect the best, not the worst."

She was right! That's when I made a shift in my thinking. *Okay, I thought, we're going to get this property. I don't know how, but I know we will.*

Then, the bigger offer fell through and the bank decided to do an online auction. I put in a bid, but the reserve wasn't met. Back to the drawing board. I wasn't fazed: the way I saw it, the bank wasn't having any luck selling "my" house to anyone else.

At that point, I started harnessing the power of visualization I'd learned from Jack and the others in *The Secret* and seeing the house as ours. When I went to work each morning, instead of simply driving by the house and looking at it longingly as I'd been doing before, I pulled into the driveway, turned off the car, then turned it on again, and backed out of the driveway, waving good-bye to Julie who I pictured waving back to me from the doorway. When I drove home from work, I pulled into the driveway again and imagined my 4 year-old son, Jake, banging through the screen door as he always did, to greet me as soon as he heard me drive up.

After a few days of this, though I was a little afraid that Julie would think I was crazy, I told her what I was doing, and asked her to join me in my visualization practice. To my delight, she agreed. The next morning, when she drove the kids to school, she pulled into the driveway, turned off the car, started the car again, and pulled out of the driveway as all of them, Julie, my 15-year old daughter Ruby, and Jake waved and called out, "Good-bye, new house! Good-bye!"

We started having fun with it. In the evenings and on the weekends, the whole family would walk down to the house—now empty—and look through the windows, claiming bedrooms for ourselves and imagining our furniture in each room. We'd sit on the back deck and look out to the horse enclosure and imagine our horse living with us again (Since we'd been renting, he'd had to be boarded at a stable nearby). Jake kept saying, "Hi new house! Hi, new house!" He loved our game.

Around that time, in the course of my work, I'd run into two women who were in Maui at a Jack Canfield training. We hit it off immediately and they recommended I read *The Success Principles*. I ran right out and purchased it.

Reading Jack's book, everything I'd read and heard came together inside me. Jack expanded my understanding of visualizations, affirmations, and goal-setting, and I saw what I'd been doing in a new light. I was already using so many of Jack's success principles:

- Take 100% responsibility for your life
- Decide what you want
- Experience your fear and take action anyway
- Reject rejection
- Practice persistence
- Keep your eye on the prize
- You get what you focus on
- Act as if (The "pretend farewells and homecomings" were in line with this one!)

I felt I was truly on track for success and my conviction level skyrocketed.

Then the bank announced a second auction. I decided to bid again, but noticed that this thought made my stomach tighten. *What was going on?* I realized I was anxious. When you purchase a house at auction, you buy it "as is." No financing clauses, no inspection clauses. You're committed, no matter what.

I'd just read Jack's principle "Release the Brakes," which helped me understand that the anxiety I felt was acting as a brake, slowing down our progress.

I told Julie, "I know it's a bit premature—especially since there's no guarantee we'll even be in the running, but let's spend the $550 to get the house inspected before the auction." So we did. At the end of the inspection, the inspector turned to me and said, "This house is in great shape. I have no reservations about it." With his words, the last bit of inner resistance left. I'd "released the brakes," and it was full speed ahead again. We went back to acting as if the house was already ours—no doubts!

What happened next surprised me. Though we went into the second auction, fully expecting to seal the deal, we were outbid!

But instead of being disappointed, I felt calm and peaceful. No matter what happened, I knew I was doing absolutely everything possible to get the house. Though my focus was incredibly high, I wasn't obsessed or attached. In fact, I felt strangely free. If it didn't work out, it meant there was an even better house in store. Nothing could discourage me!

Then the bank called again. The higher bid had fallen through. "But, Dan," Carlos said, "can you come up even a little bit? Sweeten the deal for us by $15,000?"

I was firm. "That's the price that's right for my family. No games—that's where we need to be."

I could hear Carlos sigh on the other end of the line. But he just said, "Okay, we'll get back to you," and hung up. I knew it was far less than they wanted.

It just so happened that at the time I needed to print some more business cards. After discussing it with Julie, I decided I should print up half of them with our current address and half with the new address— another big "Act as if" to show the universe we were set on that house.

When I finished printing off the cards on my computer, I put them on the kitchen counter. Julie looked through the stack of cards, and then turned to me, "You made a mistake. ALL of these cards have the address of the house down the street on them."

I smiled at her. "No mistake. I did that on purpose. We're going to be living there."

She rolled her eyes, saying, "You're crazy to—" but her sentence was interrupted by my cell phone ringing. I looked at the screen. It was Carlos.

I picked up. "Dan," he said, "I can't believe it. The bank just verbally accepted your offer. The house is yours!"

Grinning, I hung up the phone and told Julie what had happened. I watched her mouth drop open, as she screamed, "I can't believe it, I can't believe it!"

"Believe it," I said and we stood in the kitchen, hugging, and laughing, and hugging some more.

We decided not to tell the kids until the contract was signed. But when we did, they were as excited and thrilled as we had been. Jake tore around yelling, "Yay! We have our new house! We have our new house!" Ruby couldn't stop beaming at us. "It worked!" For me there was another level of satisfaction: besides the obvious prize of getting the house, we'd demonstrated to both kids how powerful their beliefs and determination can be.

We closed on our "half-price-act-as-if house" last week. I say "half-price" because just the other day, the house next door to our new house was listed at 1.4 million dollars!

After the closing, we walked around the house and yard feeling really good about it, talking about what where we were going to put the furniture, and what we'd do to the garden, in the same way we'd been doing for months—except this time it was really ours!

Julie took the kids back to the rental house and I stayed behind. Sitting alone in the house, I couldn't get over the feeling of comfort and certainty that I experienced. I felt so at home, as though the house had picked us and had been just waiting for us to move in.

It's like Jack says, "Everything you want also wants you. But you have to take action to get it."

I can't wait to apply these principles to my other goals!

TOPPING OFF
YOUR CONFIDENCE TANK

Sean Gallagher

I've always been a fairly confident guy, but I think confidence must be continuously maintained.

It's a bit like eating a meal. You come out of a restaurant full, but that doesn't mean you won't ever need to eat again. To be confident, you need to listen to other confident people. You need to be inspired. You need to be continuously motivated. That's what happened to me.

In 2008, I was the CEO of Smarthomes, Ireland's largest home technology company, a company I had cofounded with my friend Derek Roddy. With a staff of seventy, we were riding the crest of a construction boom and were installing our product in new homes across the country. Our business won numerous awards for innovation. I was well known as a successful, self-made, start-up entrepreneur.

But Ireland was beginning to experience a critical downturn in the economy. Media negativity percolated into communities and individuals. It was an era of doom and gloom.

So one Saturday I attended a seminar in The Round Room of the Irish Mansion House, home of the Irish Lord Mayor. Jack Canfield was speaking and it literally was bums-on-seats from all over Ireland, north and south. An impressive venue for a powerful presenter.

I'd read *Chicken Soup for the Soul* books and was already a great believer in the power of story to illustrate and inspire. I was immediately captured by Jack's authenticity, his content and delivery—and how he wrapped his messages and points in personal stories. He was a guy who cared, truly cared.

This is the sort of message Ireland needs, I thought. It was the sort of inspirational and activating message I wanted to spread. At the time, I was being asked to talk in schools and colleges to business students, to speak to fellow entrepreneurs, to coach and mentor. And I knew Jack was the man to mentor me.

During break, I approached him. "I'd love to learn more about what you do. I'm really open to learn. Is there somewhere you can train me?"

He gave me a card listing upcoming events, and that's how I got myself over to the States to attend Jack Canfield's Breakthrough to Success Training in Arizona.

It. Was. Phenomenal.

During my life, I'd dealt with disability and been unemployed. I'd overcome adversity. Through it all, I kept a positive frame of mind. I'd read books, studied personal development and growth, and been committed to life-long learning. But BTS took me to a whole new level. I watched Jack's mastery as—with more than 400 people in the room—he created an atmosphere for accelerated personal growth. I watched his use of experiential training as he took individuals, pairs, or small groups through exercises. I observed the impact of group dynamics on breakthroughs and found it all fascinating.

One of the points Jack emphasized repeatedly was the power of goal setting and focus to take your life to the next level. With that in mind, I set myself some serious goals, including reinventing my business, which had begun to falter in the economic downturn, and then finding someone to replace me as CEO so that I could carve out a new career. I wanted to reinvent myself as well.

According to Jack, it's never too late to find your Core Genius and to live your passion. I loved setting up businesses and mentoring others. Now I was ready to bring this core passion to the surface: Teaching and training, supporting others, and speaking.

Jack's own story resonated with me. He'd been a schoolteacher and trained in counseling and was able to go on with confidence to build such an organization and create such a degree of inspiration in people's lives . . . . I felt that, given my own varied background, I had a similar foundation from which to build. And like Jack, I could take action. I could take risks. I could change direction.

After BTS, I returned home—excited and with a renewed sense of purpose—to fulfill my goals.

Within a short time, I was able to make the necessary changes at the company to remain competitive. Derek and I even developed a new energy-saving product which garnered awards and further established our company's reputation as a cutting-edge force in the industry.

Replacing myself took a little longer. As I searched for the right person to take over my duties, I kept my goal of becoming a speaker and trainer front and center. It all kept coming back to confidence, confidence to accept the next challenge, and to take the next step.

Then, about three months after attending Breakthrough to Success, I was approached by television producer Larry Bass, to participate as an Investor in the Irish production of "Dragons' Den," the Irish version of the popular American television program, "Shark Tank." This was a fantastic opportunity! Besides further honing my speaking skills, it was an avenue to support and mentor emerging entrepreneurs.

Yet, I knew this would take some adjusting on my part. It's a bit like altering your exercise routine. If you're good at running and somebody sets you to lifting weights, you may be fit, but you're fit for a different activity. I was quite fit at running a medium-sized business. But in terms of coaching and teaching and mentoring, those muscles needed to be exercised. Developed. My work on "Dragon's Den" gave me the experience to move confidently along the new path that was opening up in front of me.

Once I found a new CEO for Smarthomes, I was free to focus full-time on my new career. So in 2010, I decided to join Jack's private coaching program, the Platinum Inner Circle, where I was surrounded by 20 other ambitious people who were focused on high-level breakthrough goals. At the end of that program, I set an objective so audacious, so daring, that I didn't share it with the group nor speak it aloud until some time later.

By then, I'd found my own speaking voice, accepting various keynoting engagements. "Dragon's Den" had built me a national profile. Across Ireland, I often urged my audiences to activation. "Step forward rather than stand back," I said.

The more I spoke at events, the more people began to ask if I would get involved in public life. "Will you step forward? Will you stand for the Presidency?"

Yes, that was my bold Platinum Goal—to run as an Independent Candidate in the 2011 Irish Presidential Election. To become President of Ireland.

It was amazing that I had the self-belief, the confidence, to tackle that.

I stood for the presidency. To do so, I implemented the success principles I'd learned at BTS: Build a key support team; speak with impeccability; act "as if."

And, with Jack as my model, I spoke authentically.

My message wasn't about politics. It was about encouraging people to look within themselves to find their strengths. To walk together. To believe in the possible. To dream and to go out there and change their own lives, to change their community, and to change the country.

I went on a "listening tour," visiting community centers, troubled youth organizations, disability groups. I heard the stories of ordinary people, I listened to everyday heroes, and I shared their thought-provoking stories everywhere I went.

In the process, I shared my personal story of overcoming the visual impairment I was born with and having the courage to start a business and create jobs. We are all faced with challenges. We can all surpass them.

Ireland needed someone to talk about adversity and hope, about overcoming unemployment and encouraging each other. At a bigger level, as a country, it needed to ask, "What is our core value? What is our core genius? What are our strengths? If we were to walk together, what could we achieve?"

I took a very simple message about hope and positivity around the country. I felt it was possible and doable and it resonated with voters. I was able to envision and act "as if." I think some people thought I was crazy. I think some humored me. But others came on board. I built a team within three months. Twenty-five hundred supporters campaigned and canvassed. In the opinion polls, I went from 2% to 4%, then up to 8% and 16%. I jumped to 28%. Four days out from the vote, I was at 40%.

Sean Gallagher for President. Let's put our strengths to work.

Throughout the campaign, I made it a point to speak impeccably. Never once did I say anything negative about other candidates. Although I came in second in the election, I kept my entire campaign absolutely positive, choosing to focus on opportunities and solutions over problems and negativity.

Most importantly to me, I had unlocked my core genius. Discovered my passion. All in all, I had taken my life to the next level. I was happy where I was, doing what I love to do.

And that brings me back, full circle, to confidence.

In 2008, I would never have imagined running for presidency. I would never have dared made the jump had I not attended BTS, had I not set goals—and walked through doors that led to new and unexpected doors for me to open.

You fill up your car with gas and you go so far, but then you've simply got to refuel again. The strategies I learned from Jack in Breakthrough to Success and subsequent programs have allowed me to continually top off my confidence.

Now, with my tank full, I'm eager to set out on the next exhilarating journey, whatever that may be.

DRESSING FOR SUCCESS

Elaine Fosse

My company, Fosse Farms, Inc., began by accident. A co-worker asked for my help with a fundraiser for the Fort Lewis Family Support Group in Tacoma, Washington. Busy working fulltime and finishing my B.A., I had no spare time to spend in the kitchen for her bake sale. Instead, I opted for the brightly-hued, homemade salad dressing I'd perfected two decades earlier. After all, family members raved over it, friends begged me to make it, and dinner hostesses always requested I bring "that marvelous dressing."

I packaged a batch of raspberry dressing in four recycled sterilized bottles, added a cute label, and topped it with a raffia ribbon. After that first bake sale, orders poured in. For the next eighteen months, I earned money for the troops by selling at additional bazaars and bake sales.

I knew I had a high-end niche product. Not only is my salad dressing great tasting, but it also meets the strict demands of consumers: It's dairy, soy, salt, gluten, preservative, and additive free. It's low in sugar and calories. And it's kosher. Obviously, I reasoned, my salad dressing was ready for a larger market. A dream began to take form. But, before I took the plunge, I wanted to test the waters to avoid becoming yet another small business statistic. I decided to sell at farmers' markets.

Unfortunately, my target markets—Bellevue, Washington and Cannon Beach, Oregon—required lots of driving, more than two hours in each direction. With school and work, it was a grueling pace. *Maybe,* I thought, *I could use the road time for research to gain insight on growing and expanding my business.*

One day, I pulled into the parking lot of Barnes and Noble

and dashed inside to do a little shopping for audio books. Jack Canfield's *The Success Principles* appealed to me, so I purchased the CD version. After listening to the first disc, I knew I was on to something. Each time I left my driveway for the long trek, I'd pop a disc into the player and by the time I reached the market, I would be energized.

The weather in Washington and Oregon is always sketchy, and more often than not made standing under a tent miserable. At times, torrential rains blew sideways as I sat on my stool, watching the water rise at my feet. But the customers kept coming. By the end of the day, I would be soaked to the bone, shivering with cold. At other times, I stood on sizzling pavement, trying to look fresh and perky in the 101-degree heat.

What a nightmare. What did I think I was doing? This mountain was bigger than me. Self-doubt, fright, and exhaustion crept in. But so did the lessons I'd learned from *The Success Principles*: Feel the fear, do it anyway. Visualize. Act as if. Go the extra mile.

Instead of giving up and giving in, I put those principles into action. I created beautiful displays. I put up great signage. I added fresh flowers to my table. I greeted every potential customer with a positive attitude and a smile. It wasn't the obstacle, I learned, but my response to the obstacle that made all the difference.

I lost count of how many times I listened to Jack Canfield's book (One CD now skips from being so well-loved). Each time, I picked up something new to inspire me, different things at different times, but always just what I needed. Like *acting as if*.

Each time I drove by Whole Foods near the Bellevue Market, I'd tell myself, "My product is going to be on these shelves." Sometimes I walked the aisles, daunted by the rows of salad dressing, and repeated it out loud, a positive affirmation in the face of so much competition.

And though it might sound as though all I thought about was salad dressing, it wasn't true. I had other dreams and goals—one of which I focused on doing my own version of Jack's Vision Board.

Honoring a long-time desire to travel to Italy, I purchased a hard-covered book on Italian villas from the Barnes and Noble sales rack. At home, I sorted through family photographs. Taking scissors in hand, I trimmed out a likeness of my son and pasted him smack into one of the book's pictures. Satisfied with the result, I added more family members—even a cutout of my car parked in front of an impressive villa on the back cover—and set the final product on the coffee table.

"What's this?" My husband laughed as he thumbed through it.

"It's my Italy book," I explained. "My Vision Book."

When friends saw it, they begged to have their pictures included. "You'll be rich and famous someday," they said. "We want to be there, too!"

"Then pick a page and give me your best pose." I snapped their photos, printed them out, and glued them to pages of the book. *We'll go. We'll all go someday after I get my product into Whole Foods.* My villa vision was wrapped up in my business vision.

Although I didn't know exactly how to get my dressings into those stores or what it would take to get it done, I refused to go into debt, hire a broker, or pay for shelf space. Instead, I expanded my line to include blackberry, cranberry, and marionberry as well as organic versions of each of them. All the while, I kept my Whole Foods dream front and center, even as I laid out money for an eye-catching label and placed my dressing in more than a dozen other stores and saw increasing online sales.

And then it happened. A message on my answering machine.

"This is Denise from the Whole Foods corporate office in Bellevue. I hear you have a product we're interested in."

My heart jumped into my throat.

It worked. It actually worked! I thought to myself. *All those principles paid off!*

Denise invited me to Whole Foods for a kind of audition. I gathered everything I'd need to make an impression and, with my heart pounding, spread out a classy, fresh tablecloth and set up to demo my product. My passion overrode my nervousness; I believe in my product and love any opportunity to share it with others.

"Seeing my dressings exclusively in Whole Foods is my goal, my dream." I handed a sample to Denise and rattled on. "I've researched the company and its vision and I really want to see my product on its shelves."

I held my breath while she tasted my dressing.

Her eyes widened. "Ohmigosh. And you have seven flavors?"

I let my own eyes drift shut in a silent, *Thank you,* but they quickly popped open again as I continued my demonstration.

With Denise as my guide and mentor, (and my little guardian angel), my dressings now stand proudly on the shelves of *all* the Washington and Oregon Whole Foods stores. Currently, we're talking about the possibility of placing it in California. My dream came true!

I often think back to the affirmations stenciled on my walls and engrained in my mind: *From small beginnings come great things. And Be all that you are capable of becoming.* They are reminders and proof positive that Jack's principles work.

Today, still passionate about Fosse Farms, I'm dreaming bigger dreams. Whole Foods nationwide? Television promotion? Adding a business partner? Whatever I decide, I know I'll get there. After all, I've gleaned the knowledge I need from hours and hours of listening to *The Success Principles.*

Meanwhile, Italy is waiting.

FINDING A WING TO CLIMB UNDER

Jonathan Kis-Lev

When I tell people that I am an artist, they look at me with a sad face, asking,

"And what do you do for a *living*?"

I answer, "It *is* my living, and it's going better than you might imagine."

Yet I couldn't have made it to this point without Jack Canfield's support—especially in the early days. Not that Jack knew me. But through his books, recordings, and films, Jack became a trusted advisor. Now, because of his work, I do what I love, travel the world, paint and experiment, and live a life I could only dream of years ago.

✦ ✦ ✦ ✦

I knew I wanted to be an artist at the age of five, when I arrived for the first day of kindergarten at my school in the Ajalon valley outside of Jerusalem, and found that I couldn't paint all day. What was the use of school if you couldn't paint?

At 19, coming back to Israel after studying art in British Columbia, I had to decide what occupation I would follow. My heart said, "Art!" Yet my mind (and my parents) said, *Study something that will get you a steady job, and do art in your free time.* I was torn.

It was then that the movie The Secret popped into my life. As I watched the film I realized that it held an awesome truth: Your thoughts become your reality. I immediately bought a copy and played it over and over while I was drawing. *Yes*, I told myself, *I can be an artist* and *make a living*.

Each time I watched the film, I found myself attracted to the white-haired man with a warm smile—Jack Canfield. So I started watching any video of Jack I could find on the internet. I also purchased the recording of his Breakthrough to Success Seminar. I listened to these CDs while I painted in the studio I shared with other artists in the industrial area of Jerusalem. In order not to disturb one another, we wore headphones. My fellow artists thought that I'd lost my mind: as I listened, I kept crying and laughing—often at the same time.

Still, during that period, I struggled to make ends meet. Whenever I reached a crossroads, when I'd think of giving up painting altogether, I turned to Jack again. At one point, I read his book, *The Success Principles*. Two of those principles caught my eye: "Success leaves clues" and "Find a wing to climb under." I realized that I needed to find a mentor: an artist who had already done what I intended to do.

Determined to follow Jack's advice, I mastered the courage to call Avi Ben-Simhon, an amazing, talented artist I admired. When he picked up the phone, I blurted out, "I'm a young artist, I'm just beginning to paint, I would really love to meet with you."

I expected him to bark at me, but after a moment of surprised silence, he said, "Sure! Can you come tomorrow?" I was so excited. I had so many questions to ask him: How should I price my paintings? What should I do with most of my time? Should I concentrate on painting, or on marketing, or on finding an agent? I really didn't know.

Avi was pleased with the paintings I showed him the next morning and said that I had a great future. Then he gave me advice that puzzled me at first, but it ended up helping take my career to the next level. Avi told me, "Price your paintings like pizza. Doesn't matter if one takes a week to finish and one takes two months. If they're both the same size, they should cost the same." From then on, it was much easier for me to price my paintings, which led to an increase in sales in my studio.

Avi also said that I should work on each painting like it's my last creation on earth. I should strive for perfection but know that a good painting never comes to completion; it only stops at an interesting place. This was freeing and made each painting feel like a step on my journey.

Two or three years passed before I read *The Success Principles* again. I had hit a bump in the road. Canvasses piled up in my studio, and no one came to see them. I had to borrow money from my parents and my friends, and I wondered if I should give up my dream. But reading Jack's words again, it was as if he believed in me, and I knew I could apply his principles to my art. I kept his book by my bedside and read it over and over. I must have read it thirty times.

Re-reading the principle of finding a mentor, I knew I was ready to find another wing to climb under. Avi was a great artist and had become a great friend, but this time I had another artist in mind, a woman who I'll call Ms. Cooper. She was like a meteor. One of Israel's most highly regarded artists, Ms. Cooper had exhibitions in museums around the world, and studios in both New York and Tel Aviv. I told myself that if she would be my mentor, she would be a huge beacon of light for my boat out there in the ocean.

I emailed Ms. Cooper, saying that I was a young artist, that I learn fast, and that it would be my honor to have her as my mentor. I didn't receive a reply. I emailed again, and still no response. I decided to call her office.

When her secretary picked up the phone, I introduced myself and asked to speak to Ms. Cooper. Her secretary said, "Are you that Kis-Lev fellow that keeps polluting our inbox?"

It was like being slapped. I was too humiliated to answer, but she didn't wait for my reply. "Listen Mr. Kis-Lev. Ms. Cooper's time is in very high demand, and she simply does not have time for any would-be artist." Then she hung up on me. *She hung up on me!* It was such a hurtful experience, especially after Avi had been so friendly and positive.

But I kept going—"feeding myself"—by listening to Jack's CDs.

Following his advice to visualize achieving my goals, I visualized Ms. Cooper as my mentor. Over the next three or four months, I read everything I could find about her and really became an expert on her work.

One of the first things I read about Ms. Cooper was her Wikipedia entry. I noticed that it was very short—only some three paragraphs about this internationally renowned artist! And though I had visualized meeting Ms. Cooper several years in the future, just a few months after my initial dismissal at the hands of her secretary, I had the thought, *What if I learned how to be a Wikipedia editor? I could contact her now and tell her I want to edit and improve her article, because it's important that people know who she is.*

For three days and three nights nonstop, I learned the ins and outs of Wikipedia language and all kinds of computer stuff. Next, I edited a few articles to test what I knew and got great responses from other Wikipedia writers. I was ready to contact Ms. Cooper.

I emailed her, saying that I was a Wikipedia editor—which I had been for about a day and a half!—and that I'd be happy to edit her article.

Within two hours, I received a phone call from her secretary. She said, "Mr. Kis-Lev? Ms. Cooper was so pleased and moved by your honoring of her, and she'd be more than happy to meet with you at your convenience. Would four hours suffice?" I told her, yes, and when she said that Ms. Cooper had just had a cancellation for the next afternoon, I said that was fine. "Good, thank you very much Mr. Kis-Lev," said the secretary, "I'm writing your name down. Hmmm . . . Mr. Kis-Lev—that name rings a bell. You must be a very well known editor!"

I was astounded, but just told her I looked forward to meeting Ms. Cooper.

I didn't realize it at the time, but I'd done just what Jack had advised in *The Success Principles*. I'd found a way to offer something of value to my chosen mentor.

The next day I arrived at the studio with my laptop and audio recorder. I was so excited, and Ms. Cooper was just amazing. She really blew my mind. She was passionate about what she did, and

I learned so much from listening to her, from just being in her presence. I left our meeting like a helicopter, flying in the air.

For the next two and a half months I worked on the Wikipedia article. After I emailed the link to the new article to her, she wrote me back and personally thanked me. I really wanted to meet with her again, so I suggested I add pictures to the article. She agreed, and I went back to her studio to take photos—it was great!

I continued to visualize that Ms. Cooper had agreed to mentor me, and about six months after we first met, I told her I wanted to write another article, one about the art movement that she takes part in. She was very happy about the idea. When we met to talk about this, she asked me, "What is it that you do, other than Wikipedia? They don't pay you, right? What is it that you do?"

I said that I was an artist.

"You're an artist and you haven't told me?"

It was funny, actually. She asked where she could see my paintings online and immediately typed in the address. She was very pleased with my work and was especially moved by the darker, black and white paintings that I did after my breakup with my girlfriend.

When I saw her reaction, I realized this was my chance. I said, "Ms. Cooper, can I ask for some advice on what I should do with my time? Some people say I should focus on developing new techniques and new styles, others say I should find an agent or focus on marketing. What should I do?"

She told me, "I'm going to give you the most important answer. This will change your life. But you will not like it."

"Okay, great, please tell me," I said.

"You're not going to like it," she repeated before adding, "You need to paint the same painting again and again and again and again. You are very talented, Jonathan, and I can see that you really like Chagall and Matisse and Picasso and Hundertwasser and Klimt. But I don't see Kis-Lev here. When you see a Van Gogh from a distance, you don't have to get close to know it's a Van Gogh. He has a signature image, and you need to find your signature image so that when people see a Kis-Lev, they know it's a

Kis-Lev. To achieve that, you need to take a favorite painting and paint it again and again. Each time you will see what you like in the painting and improve it in the next one. But you have to do it with one painting."

This was devastating advice, because what I loved in being an artist is the freedom to experiment with styles and mediums . . . But Jack teaches that mentors don't want their time wasted, and if you ask for advice, you better follow it. So, for the next eight or nine months, I locked myself in my studio and painted the same view out of my balcony, again and again and again.

And Ms. Cooper was right. I slowly developed a style that can be called a signature image. Friends tell me now that they've seen paintings in Tel Aviv or Toronto or Berlin that they knew from far off were mine. I am painting true Kis-Levs!

I wouldn't have reached that phase—I'd still be an amateur—if I hadn't met Ms. Cooper. And I wouldn't have met her if I hadn't followed Jack's advice to find a mentor.

After I finished all those paintings, I knew that I was ready for the next phase, which was to sell paintings not only through my studio, but also through galleries. I put photos of them on CDs and sent them to about thirty galleries in Israel. A month later, having received no replies, I started to call each one to ask if they would carry my work. I did this over a period of a few weeks, because it was just too difficult to do all at once. Everyone said, "No." I heard, "You're too young," "Your work is too colorful," "We only do abstracts," whatever. Some just said, "No, thank you." After I called the twentieth gallery, I told myself I had to finish, I had to reach the thirtieth gallery, but I wondered if I should give up after that. Avi was very encouraging, Ms. Cooper was very supportive, but dealing with these gallery owners was another story.

I knew from reading the "Reject Rejection" chapter in *The Success Principles* that Jack had been rejected over 140 times before he found a publisher for his first Chicken Soup book. So I kept telling myself I had to continue. By the time I called the last gallery, I felt happy to be finishing the chore.

On that call I said the same thing that I'd said to all the other gallery owners, but this time, instead of hearing, "No," I heard the lady saying, "I remember your CD. You have interesting work, but I need to see it in person. When can you come?"

My father helped me schlep some paintings to her gallery. I could see that she wasn't thrilled, but she kept two of them. She also advised me to switch from acrylic to oil paint, saying my paintings would look better with oil.

After two or three months my paintings hadn't sold, and she asked me to take them back. But her encouragement and advice made me willing to try painting with oil, and this pushed my work to a new, far more powerful level. It was the next step in my development.

Though it hasn't been an easy path, I'm making it work. Today, at 27, I'm considered one of the leading young artists in Israel, with paintings in eleven galleries, both in Israel and around the world. Last year, I was the youngest artist to sell in a public auction—a big step because this established market prices for my art. Not long ago, my paintings were shown in a world exhibition of naïve art held in Poland, and the National Bank of Israel just bought fifteen pieces of mine.

I know I still need to keep walking, but my road is paved. When I talk to young artists now, which I love to do, I tell them that no matter what anyone says, they should "go for it anyway!" And I always share what I learned from *The Success Principles*: the importance of a mentor, clearly defined goals, and persistence—always persistence.

FINDING ME . . . AND MIA

Michelle J. Kaplan

There's nothing like a spin around the dance floor with cancer as your partner to kick-start your dream machine. Looking your own mortality squarely in the eye, you can't help but ask yourself, "What am I waiting for?"

I found myself in that exact situation in 2005. At age 37, I was divorced, childless, and a breast cancer survivor. Good times.

My marriage had ended two years earlier—no big drama, my husband and I had simply grown apart. Then, a year after we split up, I was diagnosed with Stage 2 breast cancer. I spent the next year going through surgery, chemo, and radiation.

Halfway through the chemo, I hit a low point. I just couldn't see the light at the end of the tunnel anymore. To rally my fighting spirit, I vowed to myself that if I got through this, I would become a mom—a long cherished dream.

With that goal fixed firmly in my heart, I made it. My treatment, which left me exhausted, both physically and mentally, put me in remission. But, I discovered at the end of my treatments, it also put me into early menopause.

Although I was grateful to have beat the odds and survived, my dream of having a baby was dead. Over. I cried, and grieved in private, but soon I dried my tears and went back to my corporate job in Human Resources, pretending that everything was okay.

A few months later, in September 2005, I took my first business trip since my cancer diagnosis. I was in Newark Airport, waiting for my flight to depart, when I noticed a bookstore. Walking in, I saw a wooden table piled high with books with bright, white covers. I made my way to the table and picked one up. A silver-haired man smiled at me from the cover as I read the title, *The Success Principles*. Something about the book attracted me and I immediately decided to buy it. An unusual act—the only thing I buy impulsively is shoes! But I thought, *I could use some success right about now.*

Sitting on the plane, I opened the book and began reading. The first chapter really struck me: Take 100% responsibility. I'd been given a second chance at life. And suddenly I realized that it was up to me going forward to create the life I wanted for myself—no one was going to do it for me. This was scary . . . and exhilarating.

I kept reading. Jack laid out the steps for creating that life. First, he said, you have to figure out what you want, what your vision is.

Picking a vision wasn't too difficult: I still wanted to be a mom—which meant adoption. But who was going to let a single woman who was also a cancer survivor adopt a child?

It was Jack's advice, "Don't worry about 'the how' when selecting your goals," that gave me the courage to go for it. If I'd thought about how to make it happen, I'd probably have given up on that dream before I even started.

Once you've decided what you want, it's time to put it down on paper as a goal—which means it has a due date. Jack recommends writing your goals on 3 x 5 index cards and reading them every day.

Sitting with my pen poised above the card, I looked into my heart and there it was. I wrote: I will be a mother by May 31, 2007. That gave me a year and a half.

Once I wrote that down, I worked backwards.

Well, I thought, *if I'm going to be a mom, I'd better have enough money to raise a child and not have to travel for work.* That meant a new job. I wrote, "I will have a new job by Dec. 31, 2005" on another 3 x 5 index card. Four months.

I'll also need a new house. Another card: I will have a new home in a good neighborhood with good schools by April 30, 2006. Eight months.

I put the cards on my nightstand, intending to read them every day, but within a couple of days they were part of the furniture.

Then I put them on the bathroom mirror, but the steam from the shower made the ink run. *Hmm,* I thought, *I need to re-think this.* Then I got it—the car! I spent a lot of time commuting back and forth to work, so I put the cards in the cup holder.

Every day when I got in the car to go to work, I read them. And as I drove the half-hour to the office I visualized my life a year from then: a new house, a new job, and a new baby.

When I got into my car to drive home, there were those cards. I'd read them over again, and spend my evening commute doing the same thing: seeing myself with a new job, a new house, and a new baby.

A week or so after I began this routine, a woman I knew at work had to unexpectedly leave when her husband got a job in Florida. She worked in the training department, which is work I love that paid enough, and involved less travel: my ideal job! I applied for the position and got it. *Man, this index card thing works!*

For my house goal, it was just a matter of looking at my salary and figuring out how much I could spend on a house. I continued to read my cards and visualize. After looking for a few months, I found the house, put in an offer, and started the mortgage procedure. The house closed on March 15, 2006, six weeks ahead of my projected deadline!

Once I'd set the house process in motion, I knew it was time to tackle my big goal: motherhood. As a single woman and a cancer survivor, I wasn't considered a good candidate. Jack's principle, Reject Rejection, became my mantra. I contacted agencies in the US, Russia, Vietnam, Korea, and China and received a unanimous "No thanks" from each and every one. I was running out of places to call.

I shared my vision with everyone. Sometimes when things weren't going well, I was sorry I had. One day, when I'd been feeling particularly discouraged, I went over to my friend's house. That week, I'd discovered that private adoptions would cost me $100K, money I didn't have, and my other plan B, foster care, wasn't a promising option. When my friend asked me how the adoption thing was going, I sighed and said, "Not so good." I really didn't want to talk about it.

But she continued the conversation, saying, "I just heard from a friend who adopted a baby from Guatemala."

My ears perked up. *Guatemala?* I hadn't tried there. I went straight home and called the woman my friend had mentioned. We talked for two hours. At the end of our conversation, she gave me the name of three agencies. I called the first one and told a case worker I was a single woman, a cancer survivor, and wanted to adopt. She said she'd connect me to the director. On hold, I waited anxiously for 10 minutes. The director came on and said, "Yes, Ms. Kaplan, you can adopt. You'll just need a letter from your oncologist saying you're in remission."

They sent me the paperwork, which was lengthy and daunting. But the part that intimidated me the most was the cost. It was significant. Where would I get that money? *Don't worry about the how,* I kept telling myself, but I left the long application on my desk, still blank.

The July 4th weekend rolled around. I was at a party having a conversation about possible ways to pay for the adoption. Someone asked me if I had any stock or stock options that I could cash in. I said no, but something in my mind wiggled around. *Wait a second. I'd been given an award in 2001 from my company—wasn't there something about stock options involved?* I'd put the award in a drawer and forgotten about it. Now I went home and found it. Sure enough, I'd been given options that would mature in 5 years. That was now! I looked up the stock price. Selling the stock would give me almost exactly what I needed: I was only $200 shy.

Excited, I sat down and filled out the paperwork and then went on to complete all the requirements in three months, which is record time. I made a goal that my child would come home with me within a year of her birth. That, I worried, would be almost impossible to pull off. It usually takes one to one and a half years to adopt.

That's when I began using Jack's Rule of 5, which simply means that every day do five specific things that will move your goal toward completion.

Each morning I would read my goal and then spend the 30-minute commute figuring out the five things to do that day to get to my goal. On the commute home, I'd ask myself, "Did I get the five things done today to get to my goal?" If not, I'd recommit to doing whatever I hadn't done and add it to the list for the next day.

This daily review kept me on track . . . and really paid off.

I met my daughter when she was three months old and was legally her mother by May 24, 2007—just over three months later. I was able to bring her home six weeks later when she was eight months old. That kind of speed is rare in the world of adopting.

Before Mia came home, I'd bought a big, pale yellow, overstuffed rocking chair with an ottoman for the nursery. Part of my visualization was to see myself, holding my baby and sitting in that yellow chair. After she arrived, I sat in that chair many, many times, holding my Mia, my little peanut, just the way I saw it in my mind. Nine years later, we still snuggle together in that chair, reading and talking. It's one of our favorite bonding places.

Each day, as I do the mundane things that moms do—taking Mia to school, going to her girl scout meetings, art class, making dinner, and so on—I look at my raven-haired girl and marvel. I could have spent my life feeling sorry for myself, and everyone would have commiserated—my hard knocks and all that—but instead, Jack's Success Principles inspired me to go for it.

My eyes well up and my heart is filled to bursting with gratitude and love. It's not how I thought I'd have a child, but I know, in my soul, this is the child I was meant to have in my life.

Mia, at 15 months, in our chair . . .

THE POWER
OF A VISION BOARD

By Sharon Worsley

One evening in October, 2006 while eating pizza on my own, in my little condo in downtown Toronto, I was watching the DVD phenomenon 'The Secret' and heard Jack talk about how he had placed a check above his bed for $100,000, which was the money he wanted to manifest within the next 12 months.

Months earlier I had thought that it would be great to go to Italy the following year to celebrate my birthday, but when I wrote this goal in my monthly planner, part of me didn't know how it would happen; at the time I was short of cash, and another part of me didn't believe it would ever happen.

So instead of letting go of the thought, I shut off the DVD and decided to make a big request of the universe; I decided to Ask, Ask, Ask (another of Jack's principles) that the next time I ate pizza it be at 1 p.m. on May 1st, 2007 (my birthday) in Venice, Italy. I really love pizza so that was a big sacrifice for me!!!

I believed it would happen, so I started to tell everyone I knew of my request. I am sure most people thought I was crazy, but I didn't care because I believed that the universe would deliver. More importantly I built my first vision board, which included a picture of the canals of Venice.

On January 2nd, 2007, I opened an email to find that someone I had met the previous August, who knew of my quest, had decided to give me a ticket to Venice with no strings attached. The email contained an itinerary to fly on British Airways. You can just imagine how thrilled I was!

When it came time to book my hotel I contacted a past coaching client who recommended a small hotel near the canal that she had stayed at. A call to the hotel resulted in finding out that the hotel was solidly booked out due to an upcoming conference.

After hearing this, I immediately went to their website and downloaded the only picture they had on the site; a picture overlooking a terrace and the canal. I placed this photo above my computer (a mini vision board) where I continued to look at it each day imagining sitting on the terrace enjoying the view of the canal. Two weeks later I called back to find out that there now was a room available. Arriving late at night I went straight to bed, after a very long flight from Toronto.

The next day I awoke excited to go out and explore my surroundings, but first decided to the open the blinds to see what the weather was like. I was stunned to see that the view from my room was the actual picture I had taken off their website. Of all the rooms I could have been staying in and all the photos that could have been taken and placed on their site, this photo was taken from my window. This really drew home the lesson on the importance of vision boards.

In April 2007 Jack was a speaker at an event here in Toronto. In a room filled with several thousand attendees I sat glued to my seat when Jack came on stage. During his entire talk I kept visualizing standing next to him as a speaker sharing the same stage with him, not knowing how or when this would ever happen. After he completed his talk the organizer announced that if anyone wanted to meet Jack they could go down to the next floor and stand in line for an autograph.

I waited patiently in line with several hundred people eager to meet Jack. Finally I was standing in front of him and as I held out my hand to shake his I uttered, "Thanks for my trip to Italy." He looked a bit perplexed so I explained my recent trip to Venice and how he was part of it. I then told him, with my heart about to jump out of my chest, that I intended to one day share the same stage with him.

As a budding inspirational speaker I had previously set a life goal to share the same platform with Jack, someone I very much admired. I am sure he hears this statement often, but that did not diminish my resolve in letting him know of my intent.

Two weeks later I was attending an international coaching conference where the presenter said that he would be inviting one person up to be coached throughout the conference on a new coaching methodology he had developed. I just knew that I had to be the one he would pick, and so when he asked for people to raise their hands if they wanted to volunteer for this special experience I was one of the first to extend my arm. I am not normally the kind of person to raise a hand, preferring for others to have the chance, but I just felt it was meant for me to be part of this moment.

And so as part of my being coached onstage I was asked about some of my personal and business goals. I could have been timid and picked some small goals, so as not to be judged by the other coaches in the audience, but instead being true to myself I stated that I wanted to share the stage with Jack Canfield.

A couple of days into the conference one of the people attending the event came to tell me that she had spoken to a producer she knew about my goal, and that this producer was interested in interviewing me for a TV series she was developing. I couldn't believe it when she told me that Jack had been interviewed for the same series. It worked out to be exactly two weeks and 30 minutes after I had met Jack. While it might have not been an actual stage, I still felt that this was great progression towards my ultimate goal.

From that simple goal of identifying what I wanted, I have gone on to be personally mentored and trained by Jack in his inaugural year long Train the Trainer program, and attend his other trainings.

I also had the opportunity to interview Jack on video about his thoughts on principles of success for my blog, where I write about *The Success Principles* and personal leadership. At one point in the interview while Jack was speaking I remember thinking *Is this really happening?*, but I quickly reminded myself that yes indeed it was because I had used the power of a vision board.

Sometime later I asked Jack if he would consider writing the foreword for my first book. He said, "Yes." Five years prior, before I had even met Jack I had made a mock up of my planned book for my vision board, and at the bottom of this 'book' I had written a few lines that I had imagined Jack would write for the actual book. At the time I envisioned only a testimonial, but in the end this was so much more than I had ever dreamed of.

THE JOY LIST

Chris Hunter

Like everyone, I have a lot of things to do in my life. Pursuing a new career, maintaining the 33 acres of forest and farmland I live on, and spending time with my family eat up most of my week. There are a lot of activities I'd like to pursue, but up until recently, I just never got around to them. Some had been pushed to the back of my to-do list for so long, I'd simply stopped thinking about them. But applying the principles I learned from Jack Canfield changed all that—and woke me up to what's truly important.

I attended Jack's weeklong Breakthrough to Success Workshop in 2011. One of the workshop activities was to make a list of the things you love to do. Jack called it our Joy List. Excited, I wrote like a kid penning his Christmas list to Santa. I jotted down item after item, including: hiking at scenic parks; listening to songs by John Denver; being with my dear friends Tim and Todd. As I wrote, it dawned on me that I hadn't done many of these things in years. Instead, I'd spent a lot of time dwelling on my life's difficulties. No wonder I'd been so discouraged lately! When Jack asked us to prioritize the items on our Joy Lists, I moved spending time with Tim and Todd near the top.

Tim, Todd, and I had become great friends after we graduated high school in 1981. We'd been like the Three Musketeers. We got together frequently and always had a blast. Todd could make me laugh so hard I couldn't breathe! But during our early thirties, life took us in different directions. When I compiled my Joy List, I hadn't spent time with either one of them in almost 16 years.

At the Canfield workshop, I decided to make reconnecting with Tim and Todd one of my relationship goals and objectives. I'd recently moved back to my hometown near Cincinnati, Ohio, and knew Tim and Todd still lived in the area. When I returned from the workshop, I began repeating my affirmations about Todd and Tim daily as part of my strategy to re-establish my relationships with them.

Then, before I even had time to look Tim up in the phone book, I ran into him at the library. I immediately invited him to lunch at my home the next day. He came over and we laughed ourselves silly. We kidded each other about our thinning hair and expanding waistlines. At one point, I reminded Tim that thirty years ago we used to call my dad "the ol' coot." Even though we were now the age my dad had been then, we felt we were too young to be called coots. Perhaps, I suggested, we could accept "cootlings!" We both had a good chuckle about that. It felt so good to be with someone I'd known for so long.

We also talked about getting together with Todd. Neither of us had spoken with him in nearly 12 years. Tim and I parted, agreeing that the Three Musketeers would start getting together again.

Spurred by my reunion with Tim, I tried to call Todd, but his number was no longer in service. Determined to find him, I got in contact with his mother—who gave me news I wasn't prepared to hear: Todd was in a nursing home.

"He's been there for the past three months," Verna said. Her voice caught. "He's dying of a brain tumor."

Dying? Stunned, I mumbled several disjointed words of sympathy. "I'd like to visit him. Would that be okay?"

"His mind is faltering," she warned, "but I think he'll remember you."

Hanging up the phone, I was so overwhelmed with sadness that tears filled my eyes. Todd was only 49. Just one year older than me. He was too young to die! I called Tim and left a message about our friend.

At the nursing home, Todd's appearance shocked me; he was a far cry from the strong young man I remembered. His thick black hair was mostly gone, the result of cancer treatments. His feet were so swollen that he couldn't walk. Even so, when I introduced myself, his eyes lit up with recognition, and to my surprise, we ended up having a fun visit. We caught up on each other's lives. I'd switched careers from being a land surveyor to presenting nature education programs at a state park, my dream vocation. Todd shared stories about his two pet dachshunds, the adventures he'd had touring around on his antique Russian motorcycle, and his close relationship with his niece. Watching her grow up had been one of the greatest joys of his life.

When it was time to go, I promised I would drop by again in a few days. "We'll order in a pizza and celebrate just like old times."

We grinned at the memory. As teenagers, the Three Musketeers spent many nights of laughter, chowing down at the local pizzerias.

But when I arrived at the nursing home three days later, I discovered Todd had had fallen from his wheelchair and injured his arm. I drove immediately to see him at the hospital, but he was groggy from pain medicine. We visited only a few minutes before he fell asleep.

Would we ever talk again? I wondered. His weakened condition concerned me. Would he live a few more weeks? Days? Hours? It hit me then how much I regretted losing touch with Todd all those years ago.

On my drive home, I stopped by Tim's workplace to give him an update on Todd. We decided to make the next visit together. When we arrived, Todd was alert and cheerful. The three of us reminisced about our adventures together, including the night Todd's sock and shoe had been sucked right off his foot, out a hole in the floorboard of his rickety old pickup truck, as we'd sped along the highway. At one point, I asked if Todd had used any chewing tobacco lately. He grinned and rolled his eyes, "No!" At 17, Todd had swallowed a giant wad of chewing tobacco when he yelled out his truck window at some teenage girls. We definitely shared some belly laughs that afternoon in the hospital.

Over the next ten days, Tim and I made individual visits to Todd. But he had taken a turn for the worse and was unresponsive. He was moved back to the nursing home to receive hospice care.

On my last visit, Todd's eyes were open, but he was still unable to respond. The nurse told me that Todd wasn't expected to live the night. I reached out and took his hand in mine. Rubbing his chest with my other hand, I leaned toward him, telling him how thankful I was for his friendship and for all the fun times we'd had together.

Two days later, Verna called to tell me Todd had passed away.

I was in San Diego attending Jack Canfield's advanced training program and I shared my story with the other course participants. What if I'd procrastinated on my Joy List? What if I'd put off reconnecting with my friend, even for a month? In my heart, I thanked Jack again for encouraging me to make those goals.

I spoke at Todd's funeral service about what a great man Todd had been, and because of all the laughter Todd and I had shared, I included a couple of funny stories about him. I explained how and why I had chosen to reach out to my old friend, and how grateful I was to have spent some time with him during the last three weeks of his life.

I ended my talk by challenging my listeners, "If there is someone that you love being with, take steps to keep them—or get them back—in your life now. Like me, I think you'll be grateful. If you delay, you may not get another chance."

As Tim and I walked out together after the service, he asked me to have lunch with him the following Monday.

"Sure," I said, smiling. I was pleased to see Jack's Joy List making a difference in one more life.

MIRROR, MIRROR ON THE WALL, WHO DO YOU ACKNOWLEDGE MOST OF ALL?

Noreen Kelty

On the sunny morning of August 13, 2011, I was on my way to Phoenix, Arizona to attend Jack Canfield's Breakthrough to Success Training. Little did I know then what a breakthrough it was going to be. I met three women in the Super Shuttle from the airport to the hotel who were also attending BTS. There was going to be music, yoga, meditation, self-awareness exercises and experiential learning. What a week this was going to be!

Towards the end of the week, I decided I needed an accountability partner. I asked Theresa, one of the women I had met on The Blue Shuttle, who lived in Nashville, Tennessee. Living in New York, I was not sure how it would work, but I was open to the possibilities. We began the following week with our daily phone call with the Rule of Five. Each day we would tell each other our five intentions for the day and report on how we did with the previous day's intentions. For two weeks Theresa kept listing the "mirror exercise" on her list. After hearing her day after day, I finally said, "I don't really need the mirror exercise. I have always had high self-esteem and self-confidence."

She replied, "Oh, that's not what the mirror exercise is about. It is about ACKNOWLEDGING yourself." I envisioned the word "ACKNOWLEDGING" in flashing lights on Broadway. I stood frozen in one spot in my kitchen and thought about my yoga teacher Janice. Sometimes, as I was leaving her class, she would acknowledge something I had overcome in my life and she would say,

"Really, you are amazing." I would walk to the car standing a little taller, recalling the event and her statement and think "Wow, that was amazing!" This was my "AHA" moment. Maybe Theresa was on to something.

Then I thought of how naturally I acknowledged and appreciated others, and how I believed acknowledgement and appreciation was so important to their success. The employees I managed, the clients I coached for successfully losing weight, the students I taught yoga, and most importantly, my children Kelly and Michael. I immediately began to add the mirror exercise to my daily to-do list and was eager to do it for 40 consecutive days as Jack had instructed. If you missed one day, you had to start over.

The first few days were uncomfortable. You had to look into the mirror and use your name. "Noreen, I acknowledge you for packing those 5 boxes. Noreen, I am so proud of you for taking a walk this morning when you really did not want to get up. Noreen, I am so proud of you for eating an apple instead of the chocolate. Noreen, I love you!!!" Those first few days I was looking in the mirror saying, "Wow, you really have very blue eyes . . . you have blue eyes like Grandpa." I would do a few days but then I would forget and would have to begin again. Finally, I realized that if I did not miss a day, then Christmas Eve would be day number 40.

I decided this would be my Christmas gift to myself. I put notes on my alarm clock and on the mirror in the bathroom where I brushed my teeth. On Christmas Eve, I celebrated 40 days. I was developing such an intimate relationship with myself and looking forward to my evening ritual so much, that I decided to keep going and see if I could do it for 365 days in a row.

I also began sharing it with my clients and saw their amazing reactions. Just as I had been, most of my clients were very uncomfortable at first. Some tried to make it a bit humorous, some were very willing, some were brought to tears, and some were simply not willing to do it. Their reactions made me realize just how powerful this exercise was. For myself and for some of my clients, the exercise went hand and hand with another one of Jack's exercises in which you say, "*My* needs are just as important as your needs," and the other person says, "Yes, they are, Noreen." Then your partner says, "*My* needs are just as important as your needs," and I would say, "Yes, they are, Theresa."

As I worked on my 365 Days, I found myself always being mindful of all the positive things I was doing. Not only was I more aware of these things, but I was also looking at myself in the mirror and deeply connecting with myself. It felt like a daily ritual of blessing and honoring myself. I moved into using what I call the "Power of the Pause"—stopping before I made a decision or answered a request and saying to myself, "My needs are just as important as your needs." This always resulted in a better decision. No anger. No resentment. No guilt. I am incorporating these lessons and strategies in my coaching practice and I am seeing better results. After I celebrated Day Number 365, I thought to myself, *Why would I ever stop?*

Imagine when you first fell in love or when your child or grandchild was born, looking deeply into their eyes with love, admiration, and respect. The vibration is so high and you are feeling amazing. There is nothing you would not do for this person, nothing you would not do for their highest good, their health and well-being. Now imagine this person is YOU. I have always considered myself a strong, self-confident person, but after passing 1600 days of the mirror exercise, along with incorporating many other Success Principles, I am attracting wonderful things into my life daily. I am moving through the list of 101 goals that I made at Breakthrough to Success almost effortlessly. The MAGIC is in the action.

I do believe the most important thing I have incorporated into my life is the Mirror Exercise or what I now call the Compassionate Mirror Ritual. I have discovered that when we connect intimately with ourselves, we honor and bless ourselves, we notice and nurture, and we live a more purposeful life with fewer attachments. When we look inside, we see that we have everything we need. We just never looked deep enough or long enough. When you fully love and honor yourself, you are able to fully love and honor everyone else.

SEEDS OF INSPIRATION

Damen Lopez

I had a hard time as a kid. My freshman year in high school, I was 4'10" and 95 pounds. I don't think a day went by that I wasn't bullied in some form or fashion. As far as I could tell, there were no teachers or adults that looked out for me or the other students. School was a miserable experience that I survived only by the grace of God and my parents' support.

Surprisingly, I grew up to become a teacher. In 1994, I started my career at Los Peñasquitos Elementary School in San Diego. Los Peñasquitos was in a high-poverty area in an otherwise fairly affluent community. It was considered the "step-child" school, at the bottom of the heap in its district. Nobody really cared about Los Peñasquitos, or its performance, because it was where all the poor kids and the "brown kids" went. I was really driven to be there as a teacher because I thought I could help change that.

My first year, I worked as a long-term substitute by day while moonlighting as a bellman at a local hotel. One of the reasons I kept my job as a bellman was because it was very important to me to be able to relate to the parents at Los Peñasquitos that had to work two jobs in order to support their family.

So the bell that rang at the end of the day acted as a reminder that the second part of my day was about to begin. Several times a week, I would leave campus around 3:30 p.m. in order to work the 4 p.m. to midnight shift at the Radisson Hotel in San Diego. For many months, especially in the summer, the job was filled with meeting interesting people who offered plenty of tips. However, as the economy began to dip, the tips went from filling the pockets of my uniform to barely filling the palm of my hand.

One night while working alone, I pulled from my pocket three one-dollar bills and lined them in a row on the top of the bell desk. These fruitless symbols of my labor inspired me to make a decision that I had been putting off for several months. I decided right then and there that the job had nothing left to offer me.

As I began to make plans to talk with my boss about resigning, a gentleman summoned me to his car and asked for my assistance with his bags. I loaded my bell cart and proceeded to lead the man to the elevators within the hotel lobby. After delivering the items to his room I said, "Is there anything else I can help you with today, sir?"

Knowing that this was bellman language for, "Could you please tip me?" the man pulled out a crisp five-dollar bill and a brand new copy of a book. Thinking that he was going to give me a book and a five-dollar bill as a bookmark, I was surprised by his offer. He said, "Here's the deal. I only have five dollars in cash. You can have the five bucks or you can have a copy of my brand-new book worth $15. But you can't have both."

I knew my answer immediately. I didn't want some book that I knew nothing about. I wanted the five dollars! However, I was raised with enough manners to say to the man, "Sure, I love to read. I'll take the book."

I thanked him and headed downstairs. Exclaiming a few choice words under my breath, I walked to my bell desk with the same amount in my pocket as before, three dollars.

Out of boredom, I sat at the desk and opened up the book that the man had given me. Immediately, I became inspired by the collection of numerous short anecdotes, poems, and writings within the pages. These stories were often about ordinary people who did extraordinary things. I can't say that it was one specific item in the book that made such a profound impact on me, but I do remember being overtaken by a desire to somehow live a life that would influence others. As someone who has always considered himself to be quite ordinary, I finished reading the book feeling as though I was entirely capable of doing something extraordinary. I thought, Why not me?

It wasn't until many months later that I realized the full significance of my experience that day. The man was Jack Canfield and the book he gave me was *Chicken Soup for the Soul*—which went on to sell more than 10 million copies and to inspire people all around the world.

Acting on my own newfound inspiration, I applied to teach fourth grade full-time, and got the position. Even so, it didn't take more than a year at that job before I was surviving on will alone. One day I walked into the staff lounge and began to just let it all out. I vented about what I thought was wrong with the kids in my class and everything else. One teacher came up to me and putting his arm over my shoulder said with a smile, "Hey man, welcome to the club!" as if to say, "Now you can be negative like the rest of us!"

I felt something twist in the pit of my stomach. Mumbling that I had to go, I walked out of the lounge into the hallway, where I stopped and stood, lost in thought. Was I going to be ordinary? Or extraordinary? After a few minutes, I told myself, *You either change your attitude or it's going to be a long, unhappy life for you.*

That was the true turning point for me. After that day, I became committed to learning what it meant to be a good teacher, and a leader that could inspire real change. I had enough experience to know that what we do in schools can transform the lives of kids. I regretted some of the bad choices I had made up till then, like not engaging my kids and making excuses. Now I made a point of being action-oriented, addressing problems head-on, and being proactive. Over the following months and years, I looked for innovative ways to handle the daily challenges of teaching and implemented them.

The "go get 'em" spirit that I had picked up from Jack Canfield's book and other authors like him provided a constant reminder that I was meant to do something important.

Five years later, I became the principal at Los Peñasquitos! It was then that I finally realized my bigger purpose: to lead by example and inspire others. This style of leadership has required me to use many of the principles that Jack talks about: being positive, getting back to the basics, picking the things that are really important and doing them in exceptional ways, and creating a culture of universal achievement.

I truly believe that all students can succeed and it's our job to make it happen. That belief has created miracles. During my tenure as principal, Los Peñasquitos Elementary School went from being the lowest performing school in the district to being one of the highest performing schools in the entire state of California.

Based on my experience at Los Peñasquitos, in 2004 I founded the No Excuses University Network of Schools, which promotes college readiness for kids beginning in elementary school. Today, I oversee a network of more than 250 schools across the country, representing more than 150,000 kids in 22 states. I have now authored two books, *No Excuses University* which is now in it's second edition and my latest, *No Excuses Leadership: Nine BOLD Choices Exceptional Leaders Make.*

While I've clearly had the help of many people along the way, I've also taken bold steps as an individual to be gutsy. I attribute much of my success to the stories I read in *Chicken Soup for the Soul* all those years ago.

All this started with one person: Jack planting a seed of inspiration in me. I passed it on to someone else, who passed it on to another person, and it began to multiply. Now that one little seed has become a huge wave of inspiration, impacting the lives of thousands and thousands of kids and their families.

Ordinary people are capable of doing *extraordinary* things—especially when they work together!

ABOUT JACK CANFIELD

Jack Canfield, known as America's #1 Success Coach, is a bestselling author, professional speaker, trainer, and entrepreneur. He is the founder and chairman of The Canfield Training Group, which trains entrepreneurs, educators, corporate leaders, sales professionals, and motivated individuals in how to expand their vision and accelerate the achievement of their personal and professional goals.

As the creator of the beloved *Chicken Soup for the Soul*® series and the driving force behind the development and sales of more than 200 *Chicken Soup for the Soul*® books, with 100 million copies sold in the United States (and 500 million worldwide in 43 languages), Jack is uniquely qualified to talk about success. Jack's nationally syndicated newspaper column is read in 150 papers. The *Chicken Soup for the Soul*® television series aired on both the PAX and ABC networks.

Jack is a graduate of Harvard, holds a master's degree in psychological education from the University of Massachusetts, and has three honorary doctorates. Over the past 40 years, he has been a psychotherapist, an educational consultant, a corporate trainer, and a leading authority in the areas of self-esteem, breakthrough success, and peak performance.

The first edition of *The Success Principles* has sold half a million copies in 30 languages around the globe. Jack's other bestselling books—*The Success Principles for Teens, The Power of Focus, The Aladdin Factor, Dare to Win, You've Got to Read This Book!, The Key to Living the Law of Attraction, Coaching for Breakthrough Success*, and *Tapping into Ultimate Success*—have sold millions of copies and have launched complementary multimedia programs, coaching programs, and corporate training programs to enthusiastic individuals and corporations.

Jack holds a Guinness World Record title for having seven books on the New York Times bestsellers list on the same day (May 24, 1998). He also achieved a Guinness World Record title for the largest book signing (held for *Chicken Soup for the Kid's Soul*).

Jack is also the founder of The Foundation for Self-Esteem, which provides self-esteem resources and trainings to social workers, welfare recipients, and human resource professionals. Jack wrote and coproduced the GOALS

Program, a video-based training program to help people in California transition from welfare to work, which has helped 810,000 people get off welfare.

Jack has appeared on more than 1,000 radio and television programs, including *Oprah, The Montel Williams Show, Larry King Live,* the *Today* show, *Fox & Friends,* the *CBS Evening News,* the *NBC Nightly News,* and CNN's *Talk Back Live,* and on PBS and the BBC. Jack is a featured teacher in 19 movies, including *The Secret, The Truth, The Opus, Choice Point, The Tapping Solution,* and *The Keeper of the Keys.*

Jack has conducted more than 2,500 trainings, workshops, and seminars—and has presented and conducted workshops for more than 500 corporations, professional associations, universities, school systems, and mental health organizations in all 50 states and 35 countries. His clients include Microsoft, Federal Express, Siemens, Campbell's Soup Company, Virgin Records, Sony Pictures, General Electric, Sprint, Merrill Lynch, Hartford Insurance, Johnson & Johnson, Coldwell Banker, Northrop, RE/MAX, Keller Williams, UCLA, YPO, the U.S. Department of the Navy, and the Children's Miracle Network.

Jack has been inducted into the National Speakers Association Speakers Hall of Fame, is a recipient of the Rotary Club's Paul Harris Fellowship, was awarded the Golden Plate Award from the National Achievement Summit, and received the Chancellor's Medal from the University of Massachusetts. He was twice named Motivator of the Year from Business Digest magazine, received the Speaker of the Year Award from the Society of Leadership and Success, and is a recipient of the National Leadership Award from the National Association for Self-Esteem.

To find out more about Jack's Breakthrough to Success Trainings, Train-the-Trainer Program, Coaching Programs, and audio and video programs, or to inquire about hiring him as a speaker or trainer, you can contact his office at:

The Canfield Training Group, P.O. Box 30880, Santa Barbara, CA 93130
Phone: (805) 881-5191
E-mail: info@JackCanfield.com
Web sites: www.JackCanfield.com
www.CanfieldTrainings.com
www.CanfieldCoaching.com

CONNECT WITH JACK RIGHT NOW!

www.jackcanfield.com/blog

www.facebook.com/JackCanfieldFan

www.twitter.com/JackCanfield

www.Youtube.com/JackCanfield

www.linkedin.com/CanfieldJack

www.instagram.com/JackCanfield_Official

FREE RESOURCES FROM JACK CANFIELD

THE SUCCESS PRINCIPLES
10-DAY TRANSFORMATION

Over 100,000 people have participated in this FREE online personal growth training and are experiencing incredible results. Now it's your turn to have Jack mentor you over 10 days and receive over 2½ hours of exclusive audio and video content — including content from *The Success Principles*. To apply its power in your life, sign up today!

www.JackCanfied.com/transformation

SUCCESS STRATEGIES E-NEWSLETTER

Claim your FREE Subscription to Jack's Success Strategies e-Newsletter loaded with powerful advice and resources to accelerate your success. When you join our Success Community, you'll be the first to know about our latest blog content, free success tools, invitations to special online events, new products, and more.

www.JackCanfield.com.com/subscribe

SUCCESS VISION BOARD APP

Our FREE Vision Board App is a fun and powerful visualization tool that will support you in reaching your goals and help put the Law of Attraction to work for you every day. We make it easy for you to create custom vision boards and fully customize them with images, affirmations, music, custom recordings, and more.

    **www.JackCanfield.com/app**

THE SUCCESS PRINCIPLES
INSTRUCTORS GUIDE

Lead your own Success Principles study group using Jack's FREE Instructors Guide—complete with reproducible handouts, forms, and the actual words to use when facilitating the six lessons Jack has personally created for you! He'll give you everything you need to do to walk others through these powerful principles.

www.TheSuccessPrinciples.com/guide

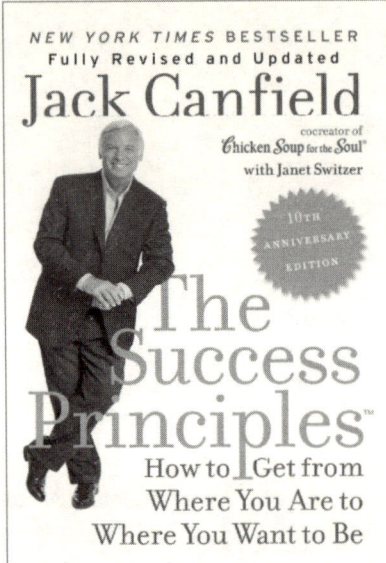

PERMISSIONS

Kabir Khan. Reprinted with permission.

Raj Bhavsar. Reprinted with permission.

Charlie Collins. Reprinted with permission.

Stephane Fournier, stephanejeanfournier@yahoo.ca. Reprinted with permission.

Romeo Marquez Jr. Reprinted with permission

John Calub. Reprinted with permission.

Forrest Willett. Reprinted with permission.

Dina Proctor. Reprinted with permission.

Lisa Nichols. Reprinted with permission.

Alicja Zajac-Merifield. Reprinted with permission.

Logan Doughty, Owner-Personal Self Protection, LLC

Mickey Sims. Reprinted with permission.

Pamela Bruner. Reprinted with permission.

Mejo Okon. Reprinted with permission.

Tresa Leftenant. Reprinted with permission.

Heather O'Brien Walker. Author, *Don't Give Up, Get Up!* and *HELPability*®
Factor | Creator of the HELP Philosophy®

Jake Ballentine. Reprinted with permission.

Jana Stanfield. Reprinted with permission.

Penny Bongato. Reprinted with permission.

Gerry Visca, Why Guy. Reprinted with permission.

JoAnn Myers. Reprinted with permission.

Kate Butler, #1 Bestselling Author & Mindset Success Coach.

Daniel Hunter. Reprinted with permission.

Sean Gallagher, Entrepreneur, Speaker & Writer. Reprinted with permission.

Elaine Fosse. Reprinted with permission.

Jonathan Kis-Lev, www.kis-lev.com. Reprinted with permission.

Michelle J. Kaplan. Reprinted with permission.

Sharon Worsley, author of *Live By Choice, Not By Chance . . . How to Wake Up, Shake
Up and Show Up in Life*. Reprinted with permission.

Chris Hunter. Reprinted with permission.

Noreen Kelty. Reprinted with permission.

Damen Lopez, Founder, No Excuses University. Reprinted with permission.

NOTES

NOTES

NOTES